THESPIS

Or
The Gods Grown Old

An Entirely Original Grotesque Opera in
Two Acts

In a new performing version
by Anthony Baker & Timothy Henty

Original Libretto by
W.S GILBERT

(Adapted and revised by Anthony Baker)

Music from
ARTHUR SULLIVAN & JACQUES OFFENBACH

Music selected by Baker & Henty

Additional music, arrangements and orchestration by Timothy Henty

E.G

Eton Grove Press
London
2009

Timothy Henty would like to thank his colleagues, friends and family for their constant and tireless support and encouragement, and in particular his wife Louise, to whom his work on this project is lovingly dedicated.

Published by Eton Grove Press
London
December 2009

ISBN 978 0 9564 6460 6

PERFORMING RIGHTS

Applications for public performance of this work should be addressed to AnthonyBaker who can be contacted via www.anthonybaker.net

Printed by Lulu.com

Contents

THESPIS; Or, The Gods Grown Old

Act I

Act II

Appendix

PREFACE

This new performing version of Gilbert and Sullivan's *Thespis* is the result of a year long collaboration between Timothy Henty and myself, which began in 2007 and culminated in three professional performances at the historic and exquisite Normansfield Theatre, Teddington on the 8th and 9th March 2008.

Whilst the original plan for the production was to use one of the existing reconstructions of the *Thespis* score, after long and careful consideration we decided that no single existing version convinced us in its entirety. So we opted to take the plunge and attempt our own version. This would include some revisions and adaptations to W.S. Gilbert's printed (but unedited) libretto, as well as supplying settings and orchestrations for all the musical numbers in the piece, apart from the two numbers which are known to survive from the original Sullivan score *"Little Maid of Arcadee"* and *"Climbing over rocky Mountain."*

Rather than composing a new score in the style of Sullivan, or indeed in any alternative style, we wanted, primarily, to try and find suitable existing music from Sullivan's output and fit that to Gilbert's lyrics. Of course we were far from the first people to have attempted a recreation of *Thespis* in this manner and when going through all the possible options for which Sullivan melody best suited the lyrics to a particular song, inevitably, it was impossible for us not to be aware of and influenced by the choices of those that had been through this process before us.

It is probably fair to say that the two recreations that were most influential on our Score were those by Ron Orenstein/John Huston for a production performed by the St. Pats Players in Canada in 1993 and above all, the version created by Selwyn Tillett and Rod Spencer in 2002 and performed as part of a presentation to the Sir Arthur Sullivan Society.

Ron Orenstein has argued strongly that the quartet *"If You Ask Me To Advise You"* from *The Rose of Persia* was possibly lifted from Sullivan's original setting of the Quartet of identity confusion in Act 2 of *Thespis*, *"You're Diana I'm Apollo."* We decided that we liked this choice, which had the added benefit that it was taken from a relatively unknown Sullivan work, so would have a novelty value for most of the audience. However we chose to set the number a little differently (you cannot simply duplicate the *Rose of Persia* setting in its entirety to fit Gilbert's lyrics in *Thespis*), and we also included something from *Patience* as part of the number.

Likewise for the Opening Chorus of Act Two, *"Of All Symposia"* we followed the Orenstein/St Pats players choice and used *"With Cards and Dice"* from *The Beauty Stone,* but again set it somewhat differently and chose another melody for Sillimon's solo.

The Tillett / Spencer version was of great interest to us and we are enormously indebted to Selwyn Tillett and Rod Spencer for allowing us access to their material, for their great support and encouragement and in particular, Selwyn's generosity in allowing us to develop some of the original ideas he either used in his *Thespis* score or outlined in the pre -performance lecture to the Sullivan Society. [1]

---

[1] The text of this lecture entitled *40 years of Thespis scholarship* is available as a PDF download via the *Thespis* pages on the internet based Gilbert and Sullivan archive

Whilst there were parts of their version that we felt we couldn't buy into, Tillett and Spencer had many brilliant ideas. In particular the arguments for use of Offenbach's music in the original Sullivan score of *Thespis*[2] and a possible double- chorus in the Act One Finale using Sullivan and Offenbach music combined.

Whilst Tillett and Spencer didn't ultimately set their Act One finale in this way, we found the idea just too good to resist and we respectfully dedicate this part of our version to them.

ACKNOWLEDGEMENTS

There are many others who played a significant role in helping bring our vision of *Thespis* to fruition but first and foremost the authors would particularly like to thank Chris Crowcroft for his skills as producer and promoter of the Normansfield production as well as being the writer of the Introduction to this Score and the lyricist behind an optional new duet for Thespis and Mercury in Act Two, *"Life on Earth's a clever toy"* which has been added to our version post - Normansfield and is to be found in the Appendix.

We would also like to thank Robin Gordon-Powell of the Sir Arthur Sullivan Society, the 2008 Normansfield Cast, Crew and Production Team, the participants of the 2007 *Thespis* Workshop, the members of the London Kensington Sinfonia and leader Sophie Ryan, James Young, Max Charles Davies, David Eaton and John Wilson.

In addition we owe our grateful thanks to The Gilbert and Sullivan Society who were generous sponsors of the production and to all those whose names we have omitted here but whose contribution we have greatly appreciated.

Anthony Baker

London

December 2009

---

[2] Also commented on by Terence Rees in his book "Thespis a Gilbert and Sullivan enigma"

First published in 1964 Dillons University Bookshop and now available from the Sir Arthur Sullivan Society. P58-59

INTRODUCTION
By Chris Crowcroft

When the curtain went up on the Baker-Henty recreation of ***THESPIS; Or, The Gods Grown Old*** on March 8th 2008 - the exact day of the year when the original show closed 136 years before - the atmosphere inside the theatre was very different from opening night on December 26th 1871.

That first, boozy Boxing Day audience which piled into the Gaiety Theatre might have thought it knew what to expect from a burlesque, albeit newly created and composed by the debut partnership of W.S. Gilbert and Arthur Sullivan. It didn't entirely get it. *The Orchestra* wrote that it was 'somewhat over the heads of the audience' while *The Observer* wrote 'the acting, as well as the business, will want working up before it can be fairly criticized.' But *The Daily Telegraph* predicted that 'few happier entertainments will be found' and *The Times* 'a high place among the novelties of the season.'

BURLESQUE

Burlesque was a speciality in this 2000 seat emporium served by a high class restaurant, programmes perfumed by M.Rimmel, with billiards and smoking rooms; the Gaiety valued a high turnover of 'extravaganza' shows which sent thousands of punters through the money-making facilities attached. It was in every sense of the word an emporium.

This wasn't the family entertainment G&S later went in for. Burlesques came out of pantomime, pastiching serious, often operatic models rather than fairytale stories. Gilbert had written several sending up Donizetti and Meyerbeer (for example *Robert the Devil*) for The Gaiety. But *Thespis* has a novel, original storyline in which the authorial voice, first heard in the topsy-turvydom of Gilbert's nonsense verse, his *Bab Ballads* from the previous decade, is clear. And the music was mostly new, even if critics heard echoes of Offenbach and whose own opéra bouffe mocking the Olympian Gods (*Orphée aux Enfers*) was well known to audiences of the day.

Even so, burlesque did not die with *Thespis,* nor indeed within the partnership between its two authors. 'For he is an Englishman' in *HMS Pinafore* and 'When Britain really ruled the waves' in *Iolanthe* could be stock burlesque numbers; and the fantasy atmosphere of many of Gilbert's plots owe much to burlesque and its antecedents.

For burlesque is an offshoot of stock comic entertainment going back centuries. True, it added theatrical effects while preserving the harlequinade (somewhat degraded according to George Bernard Shaw, who was a great devotee). But the stock characters and situations borrow from Commedia dell'arte which spawned opera buffa, operetta and singspiel. And Commedia dell'arte comes from the late mediaeval comedy interludes, which in England's public theatre included post-play jigs, bawdy song and dance confections in which Shakespeare's chief clown, Will Kemp specialized.

THE SITUATION IN 1871

Of the two authors, working together for the first time – they had been introduced two years before at a rehearsal of Gilbert and Clay's *Ages Ago-* the young Arthur Sullivan, not yet thirty, had the more established profile in the public eye. With a symphony, cantata, suites of incidental music, successful song and hymn settings already to his credit, he was the great musical hope of the British musical establishment.

Older by six years, Gilbert was not yet entirely settled in his career. He had been by turns a magazine contributor (his *Bab Ballads*), drama critic, student stage director and tyro dramatist and librettist. His burlesques, of which *Thespis* was the latest and most ambitious, were, in economic terms, jobbing work – he was paid £600 for it. His straight theatre work was developing in parallel. In fact, only a few days before the opening at the Gaiety, his play *Pygmalion and Galatea* had opened in the West End. It was his first great success, transferred to New York and in his lifetime made him £40,000 (£3m in modern terms). None of this could have been foretold in the autumn of 1871.

In retrospect, Gilbert had mixed views about *Thespis* – 'in no sense a failure although it achieved no considerable success,' he said thirty years after. This was hindsight and hardly comparing like with like, viz a viz the hundreds of performances per production for the more mainstream G&S repertoire; burlesque was more ephemeral.

What would have annoyed him were the practical conditions – rehearsals were restricted to what he could quarry within a two week period, the first of which saw J L Toole, the star, absent on tour; the rest of the cast were available mornings only due to other calls. It is likely that the Gaiety's regular stage manager, Robert Soutar, married to its female star, Nellie Farren, had more of a hand in stage direction than Gilbert wanted. Gilbert lacked the full control he insisted on later with D'Oyly Carte.

Even so, the show settled down (after cutting), achieved even better press (about the third night, the *London Figaro* wrote that 'not a single hitch is now to be perceived in the performance......evident delight of the audience from beginning to end'), ran on time and into March for 64 performances; good business for a Christmas piece, the Gaiety's impresario thought. When Hollingshead's rival, Carte, after the success of bringing G&S back together for *Trial by Jury* asked if *Thespis* could be revived for Christmas 1875, Gilbert had no hesitation in accepting the offer provided the authors could rework it. Carte's backers did not put up the money. It was *The Sorcerer* which followed.

THE PERFORMERS

The original company were the stars of the Gaiety Theatre in The Strand under the impresario, 'Practical John' Hollingshead. His main attractions were the comedian JL Toole (who was employed at £100 a week; £7500 in today's terms) who played the actor-manager Thespis – he was a bosom friend of Henry Irving, then just beginning to make his mark at the Lyceum; and 'the best girl-boy' of the age, Nellie Farren. As befitted the Gaiety, Toole had a much broader style than George Grossmith who later created most of the G&S comedian roles. He had his own catchphrases which Gilbert was required to allow for in the script ('don't know ya, don't know ya' for example). What is clear is that the Gaiety Company was clearly more settled into this broader, burlesque style than the younger, more flexible ensembles which Gilbert and Sullivan later recruited.

Nellie Farren was a versatile actor-dancer from an acting family spanning four generations, with a vaudeville style. She specialised in comedy travesti (breeches/tights) roles, and if she had a scrap of a voice, she had a petite physique and 'the best legs in the business.' She played them for 25 years until ill-health forced her retirement from the stage. An ill-advised venture into theatre management dissipated her savings. She was rescued by a benefit led by WS Gilbert which filled Drury Lane and raised, in modern terms, half a million pounds to fund the last few years of her life (she died, between Sullivan and Gilbert, in 1904, the hearse followed by 5000 people to the grave).

The supporting role of Apollo was played by Arthur Sullivan's brother Fred who went on to create the role of the Judge in *Trial by Jury*. His premature death (memorialised by his brother in *The Lost Chord*) gave George Grossmith his chance to create most of the comic leads which followed. The leading ladies were Constance Loseby (Nicemis) who had opera in her background and Annie Tremaine, (Daphne) who came from the music halls before going on to tour in the USA where, given wider operatic scope, she 'caused a sensation.' JG Taylor, who played Sillimon, the stage manager, crops up again in the history of G&S – he took on the part of Sir Joseph Porter in the rival production of *HMS Pinafore* created by the disgruntled backing syndicate ousted by D'Oyly Carte mid-run; he apparently played the part 'as a low comedian.' The versatile Robert Soutar played the (supposedly reformed) drunkard Tipseion – his partnership with Farren did not last. The Payne brothers, Harry and Fred, experienced pantomimists from a notable dance-mime family (their father was the company's ballet master), played Preposteros and Stupidas. By no means least, Mlle. Clary from Belgium played the leading juvenile male en - travesti, Sparkeion. She chose *Thespis* for her lucrative benefit that season.

MODERN REVIVALS

Because the musical score has long been lost, as well as the final performing libretto (we have Gilbert's author's draft only), there have been more than twenty attempted reconstructions of the work in the second half of the 20th century. Of greatest note in Britain, Terence Rees and Garth Morton paved the way in 1962 with a performing version first presented by amateurs from the Opera Group of London University. In 2002 Selwyn Tillett and Rod Spencer presented to the Sir Arthur Sullivan Society a semi – staged version performed by a mix of amateurs and professionals.

In this version they put forward the hypothesis that there is more of *Thespis* in *Pirates of Penzance* than had previously been supposed, in addition to the known ensemble *Climbing over Rocky Mountain.* This, with the song *Little Maid of Arcadee* is all we can be sure was in the original score. In addition in 1990 Tillett and Spencer had claimed to have identified the original Ballet music for *Thespis* whilst working on preparing a performing edition of two of Sullivan's ballets, *L'Ile Enchantée* and *Victoria and Merrie*

England. They included some numbers from this in their new version but did not include a Ballet as part of their staging.

The choice appears to be between re-using real Sullivan, or composing anew. Further afield, Ron Orenstein, Tom Petiet and Roger Wertenberger in Canada and the St Pats Players have put forward their versions, as has Bruce Montgomery (pastiche Sullivan score), with the Savoy Company of Philadelphia .

BAKER-HENTY

This edition was the original inspiration of opera designer and director Anthony Baker, in collaboration with the conductor, arranger and composer, Timothy Henty. In 2007 Baker relaunched, for professional performance, the unique and exquisite Normansfield Theatre in Teddington, London. His choice of production was *Patience* by Gilbert & Sullivan, assisted by the Carl Rosa Opera Company. The production was conceived as a recreation of the Victorian style of presentation, with the first act re-scripted by the writer of this Introduction as if the original company was in rehearsal at Normansfield.

The Assembly Room at Normansfield was opened on the 27th June 1879 in their sanatorium by Dr and Mrs John Langdon Down, he being the first identifier of Down's Syndrome. The original production of *HMS Pinafore* was still running at the time at the Opera Comique. At Normansfield, notable performers were recruited from the London stage to add 'tone' to the audience for in house performances. George Grossmith, star of Gilbert & Sullivan was one such.

The theatre saw no public performance after 1909 although it continued in private use. In 2000/01 it was restored by John Laing Homes as part of the residential redevelopment of the site. It retains a unique collection of original Victorian painted scenery. The ancestor portraits in the main hall are by Ballard from Act 2 of *Ruddigore*, the original 1887 production, acquired at sale from Richard D'Oyly Carte in the 1890s.

Such was the success of *Patience* that the production team decided to reconstruct and remount *Thespis*, with orchestra, and a fully professional cast. It ran for three sold-out performances (drawn from a 200 mile radius) on March 8/9th 2008.

The production was heavily previewed in/on the *Daily Telegraph, London Evening Standard, Time Out, BBC & TV Radio News.* A surprise guest was film-maker Mike Leigh, director of *Topsy-Turvy*.

Opera commented 'an excellent pit band under Henty's vivacious baton, and Baker directed an amusing production.....a delightful little show with considerable curiosity value.' It added that 'the performing edition has been sensitively and intelligently prepared.....the solutions work nicely, and could well establish themselves as a template.'

Let's hope so!

A NOTE ON THE SCORE
By Timothy Henty

All the principal musical material in this version of *Thespis* originates from the scores of Sir Arthur Sullivan, and occasionally from the score to *L'Orphée aux Enfers* by Jacques Offenbach. From our initial research we were aware that Sullivan's score to *Thespis* clearly included some recognizable music by Offenbach, and after studying his works, it transpired that there seemed to be a specific textual link between *L'Orphée aux Enfers* and Gilbert's libretto for *Thespis*. For example, in setting Gilbert's text "Goodness gracious, how audacious, Earth is spacious, Why come here?" (when mortals are seen climbing Mount Olympus), we chose to use the music for *Il s'approche, Il s'avance* from *L'Orphée aux Enfers*, in which opera another mortal – Orphée – is also seen climbing Mount Olympus. The music in both cases is sung by the same characters: The Gods. This seems to be true to the contemporary style of burlesque composition at the Gaiety and also demonstrates what we feel is Gilbert's clear parody of sections from *L'Orphée aux Enfers* within the plot of *Thespis*.

Anthony Baker and I worked in collaboration to choose music for our score principally by selecting melodies that fit the scansion of Gilbert's text, and therefore primarily chose compositions that were rhythmically and metrically suitable. However, we also felt it important to consider the nature of the chosen music, how it affected the tone of the text, and how the choice of music emotionally related to the characters and dramatic situations within the Opera. We hope that the combination of these three elements have helped us to create a score that at least pays tribute to Sullivan's celebrated talent for text setting.

When approaching the names of the characters and how to set them to music, we took advantage of Gilbert's deft way with words. Nicemis, for example, could be a two or a three syllable name depending on your view. The dubiously Grecian pronunciation *'nigh-See-miss'* is an obvious play on *'nice miss'*: the latter a comically transparent reference to the character's persona and, we felt, the right choice for us. In the same manner, Sparkeion becomes the two syllable *'Spark-yun'* – a rather typically Victorian diminution of 'sparky one'. We set both names as two syllable words within the score and intend for them to be pronounced in the same manner during the spoken dialogue. Tipseon; Timidon; Sillimon and the rest – again rather hopeless character references – were obvious as three syllable names.

We assigned vocal registers with respect to the original casting, and the research that has been undertaken in ascertaining what manner of voice each singer in the 1871/2 cast possessed. Two characters are worth a mention here: Mercury and Sparkeion. In the original production both were portrayed by female performers dressed as men 'en travesti'. This concept is still relatively common considering the principally British pantomime tradition and its use of female performers to play young male characters, such as Aladdin or Dick Whittington. Indeed, we also see the reversal of that concept with (usually well known) male performers portraying stock characters such as Widow Twankey. As *Thespis* was originally conceived within this tradition, we made the decision to maintain the concept and to cast female performers in both roles in our 2008 production. On reflection, we remain convinced that the Puck-like Mercury is best performed 'en travesti' but realise that some (either through artistic choice or necessity), may prefer to cast Sparkeion as a male tenor. Whilst we hope that some prospective producers will look upon casting Sparkeion 'en travesti', as an interesting and historically correct challenge, we leave the decision open to directors and conductors and trust that the vocal ranges used in the score facilitate the casting of a male tenor if so desired.

In a very small number of circumstances I found it necessary to compose music in order to create linking passages, or to provide development or completion where the chosen source material did not perfectly fit Gilbert's text. In almost every case those 'compositions' are – out of respect for Sir Arthur – illusions, as I tried in these cases to adapt material from his work to fit the situation. In *Here far away*, for example, the introduction and the coda are derived from *The Pirates of Penzance* and *HMS Pinafore* (though still involving the principal source material of the piece: Sullivan's song *The Chorister*), whilst the closing vocal phrase of the same piece is an adaptation of music from *The Gondoliers*.

Reworking source material occasionally provided me with irresistible opportunities to create musical allusions to Sullivan's more established works. Some may call these 'in jokes' (although any humour present is a little strained for my taste). The opening instrumental bars of our Finale to Act I employ a harmonic progression taken from *HMS Pinafore*, where Sullivan sets Gilbert's line "…his trusty heart and brown right hand": positive attributes that Jupiter erroneously believes Thespis owns when he entrusts Mount Olympus to him. Avid readers will discover other such moments in the score.

When performing this version, I would strongly encourage both singers and my colleagues on the podium to use imagination by trying to approach each musical section as if it had originated from *Thespis*. I acknowledge that this is a challenge for G&S enthusiasts who are familiar with the music as it is sung in its original state, but when I conducted the piece at Normansfield I often felt it necessary to choose a tempo or style of phrasing that I would not normally consider in a performance of the original material. To this effect, I have kept tempo and dynamic markings to what I would call – for Sullivan – a typical minimum throughout the score, and have been more specific only where I have felt it necessary to explain tempo relationships or style within context.

Finally, it is inevitable that fresh eyes will spot errors on my part in the engraving of the score. I hope that they are not numerous and that performers can easily correct them. Opinions on our musical choices and text setting are of course subjective, but if you happen to spot an obvious wrong note or a passage that is unsightly in its layout, I would be most grateful to hear of it. I can be contacted via my website: www.timothyhenty.com, and if we should ever create an updated edition of this publication, I will eagerly consider your comments.

Timothy Henty
Surrey, England
December 2009

NOTES ON THE ORIGINAL LIBRETTO
By Anthony Baker

Unlike Sullivan's score, W.S. Gilbert's libretto for *Thespis* has survived, and has been printed many times in various books and collections of Gilbert's works. However these texts have always derived from the first edition made available for purchase by audiences at the Gaiety Theatre in 1871/2, and herein lies a problem for those intending to stage *Thespis*.

As pointed out by Terence Rees,[1] this first text is clearly un-proofed by the author as it is full of errors. Crucially it also seems to omit lines of dialogue quoted verbatim by critics who attended early performances. The conclusion must be that this text remained an early draft copy of the libretto and that in the rush to produce *Thespis*, the printer's deadlines precluded Gilbert making substantial revisions if the copy was to be made available for sale to the public on opening night.

The work was to be included in a complete edition of Gilbert's plays published by Chatto & Windus in 1911,[2] but unfortunately Gilbert died before the proofs were ready and again it was the unedited 1871 text (with some spelling mistakes corrected) which was used.

LIBRETTO FOR THE NORMANSFIELD PRODUCTION

Knowing that Gilbert wanted to revise certain aspects of *Thespis* for the proposed revival in 1875 was the key to my freedom to create a revised edition for performance at Normansfield. Certain practicalities forced me, in any case, to look at the number of characters involved since we were limited by budget and a small stage to a maximum cast of thirteen and no chorus.

The most evident revision is the cutting of the two characters originally played by the Payne brothers, *Stupidas* and *Preposteros*. In re-reading their scene and having seen it performed by others in various amateur productions, I could not believe that, however competently performed, their dialogue would be comprehensible and amusing to a modern audience. Their lines seem to be written simply to allow them to play stock characters from the Victorian pantomime and to give them a chance to perform some of their trademark slapstick routines.Thereafter they play no noticeable role in *Thespis* and are not in any way material to its plot.

---

[1] Rees, Chapter 7 pp90-94
[2] W.S. Gilbert *Original Plays*, Fourth Series, London 1911

Whilst there is no doubt that this was an important feature of the Gaiety at the time and in the type of Christmas Extravaganza which *Thespis* was conceived to be, I couldn't help wondering if Gilbert might have opted to cut this element of the piece if the planned 1875 revival at a different theatre (the much smaller Criterion) had taken place.

In addition, the role of *Sillimon* is curiously underwritten in Act One. Assuming the original libretto is correct on this score, he has all of two lines. Yet in Act Two he becomes a much more significant character with a solo in the opening chorus and substantial dialogue scenes with other leading characters. I considered it helpful to expand his character in Act One as a much put-upon and undervalued stage manager, by allocating some of Stupidas's and Preposteros's lines to him, and adding one or two of my own.

The character of *Mars* is slightly expanded in this version. Again, he is seriously underwritten in the original and seems to be there merely to supply the tenor line in the Gods' ensemble numbers. Developing a personality based on the one or two lines which Gilbert wrote for him, I attempted to expand his character into a crusty, senile and rather deaf Victorian colonel.

Taking my cue from Terence Rees's reconstruction, I included part of a scene which is recorded as taking place by Victorian critics, in which Thespis is introduced to the (less than alluring) Goddess *Venus*. However, at Normansfield these lines were instead allocated to *Diana* – and worked very well - but they could easily be restored to Venus, creating a small cameo role opportunity.

There are a few extra jokes in this script, some of which I can claim credit /blame for and some of which came out of the workshop/rehearsal process and my colleagues.

Inevitably when setting the existing lyrics to melodies from other works by Sullivan we felt it sometimes necessary for the sake of scansion/singability to omit or change the order of certain words, and we feel certain that this is, in any case, likely to have happened in the original score. Very occasionally we replace Gilbert's text with an alternative, either from another Gilbert work or newly written. For example when the angry Gods can take no more of Thespis's incompetence in the climax of the Olympian courtroom scene in Act Two, we replace *"We can't stand this"* etc. with *" With fury deep we burn "* from *Utopia Limited.*

As in all things theatrical, the ultimate judge of whether these modifications are deemed a success is the audience, and this writer can only report that the reaction at Normansfield was overwhelmingly positive.

SYNOPSIS

The Gods on Mount Olympus are growing old. Diana, Goddess of the Moon feels the cold at nights, Apollo the Sun God finds it difficult to get up in the morning, Jupiter's thunderbolt is not what it was. Mercury, messenger of the Gods complains that if it wasn't for him nothing would get done.

A picnic party of actors led by their manager Thespis is spotted climbing the slopes of the sacred mountain. Interrogated by the Gods, Thespis avers that the Gods are out of touch and advises them to go on tour to earth to reconnect with their public. The actors will deputise for them, advised by Mercury who will remain behind. The Gods agree.

Act Two finds Thespis and his deputy Gods well pleased with themselves. Mercury complains that they don't know what they are doing, especially since every deputy has been cast against type – Mars is now Timidon who has the character his name suggests. There are relationship mix- ups amongst the company as a result of their mythological pasts. And every deputy God has been encouraged to experiment, which destroys the calendar, ruins viniculture and upsets international relations (by abolishing War!). As earthly petitions threaten to overwhelm the new order, the original Gods return appalled. They retake their positions and send the actors back down to earth.

✷

THESPIS
DRAMATIS PERSONAE.
& Vocal Requirements

THE GODS.

JUPITER...*Bass*

APOLLO..*Baritone*

MARS..*Tenor*

DIANA...*Contralto*

MERCURY...*Mezzo-Soprano*

MORTALS.

THESPIS ....*Baritone*

SILLIMON...*Baritone*

TIMIDON...*Tenor*

TIPSEION...*Spoken Role*

SPARKEION.................................*Mezzo-Soprano or Tenor*

NICEMIS..*Soprano*

PRETTEIA...*Soprano.*

DAPHNE..*Mezzo-Soprano*

CYMON...*Spoken Role*

Chorus of Weary Stars, Aged Deities & Members of Thespis's Theatrical Company.

Synopsis of Scenes

Act I.- *Ruined Temple of the Gods on the Summit of Mount Olympus.*

Act II.- *The Same, "Theatrically" Restored One Year Later.*

Dramatis Personæ.

	Gaiety Theatre 1871	Normansfield Theatre 2008
The Gods		
JUPITER *(Aged Deity)*	Mr John Maclean	Mr Simon Masterton-Smith
APOLLO *(Aged Deity)*	Mr Fred Sullivan	Mr Ian Belsey
MARS *(Aged Deity)*	Mr Frank Wood	Mr Ted Schmitz
DIANA *(Aged Deity)*	Mrs Henry Leigh	Ms Jill Pert
MERCURY	Miss Ellen 'Nellie' Farren	Ms Rebecca Seale
The Mortals		
THESPIS (*Manager of a Travelling Theatrical Co.*)	Mr J L Toole	Mr Richard Suart
SILLIMON (*his stage manager*)	Mr J G Taylor	Mr Giles Davies
SPARKEION	Mlle Clary	Ms Miranda Westcott
TIMIDON	Mr Marshall	Mr David Menezes
TIPSEION	Mr Robert Soutar	Mr Martin Lamb
NICEMIS	Miss Constance Loseby	Ms Rachel Harland
DAPHNE	Miss Annie Tremaine	Ms Melanie Lodge
CYMON	Miss L Wilson	Ms Sian Jones
PRETTEIA	Miss Rose Berend	Ms Sian Jones
Director	Mr W S Gilbert & Mr Robert Soutar	Mr Anthony Baker
Conductor	Mr Arthur Sullivan & Herr Meyer Lutz	Mr Timothy Henty
Choreographer	Mr W H Payne	Ms Caroline Pope

Thespis; Or, The Gods Grown Old first performed at the Gaiety Theatre, London, England, on 26th December 1871.
This version first performed at the Normansfield Theatre, Teddington, England, on the 8th March 2008.

THESPIS
Or
The Gods Grown Old

INTRODUCTION

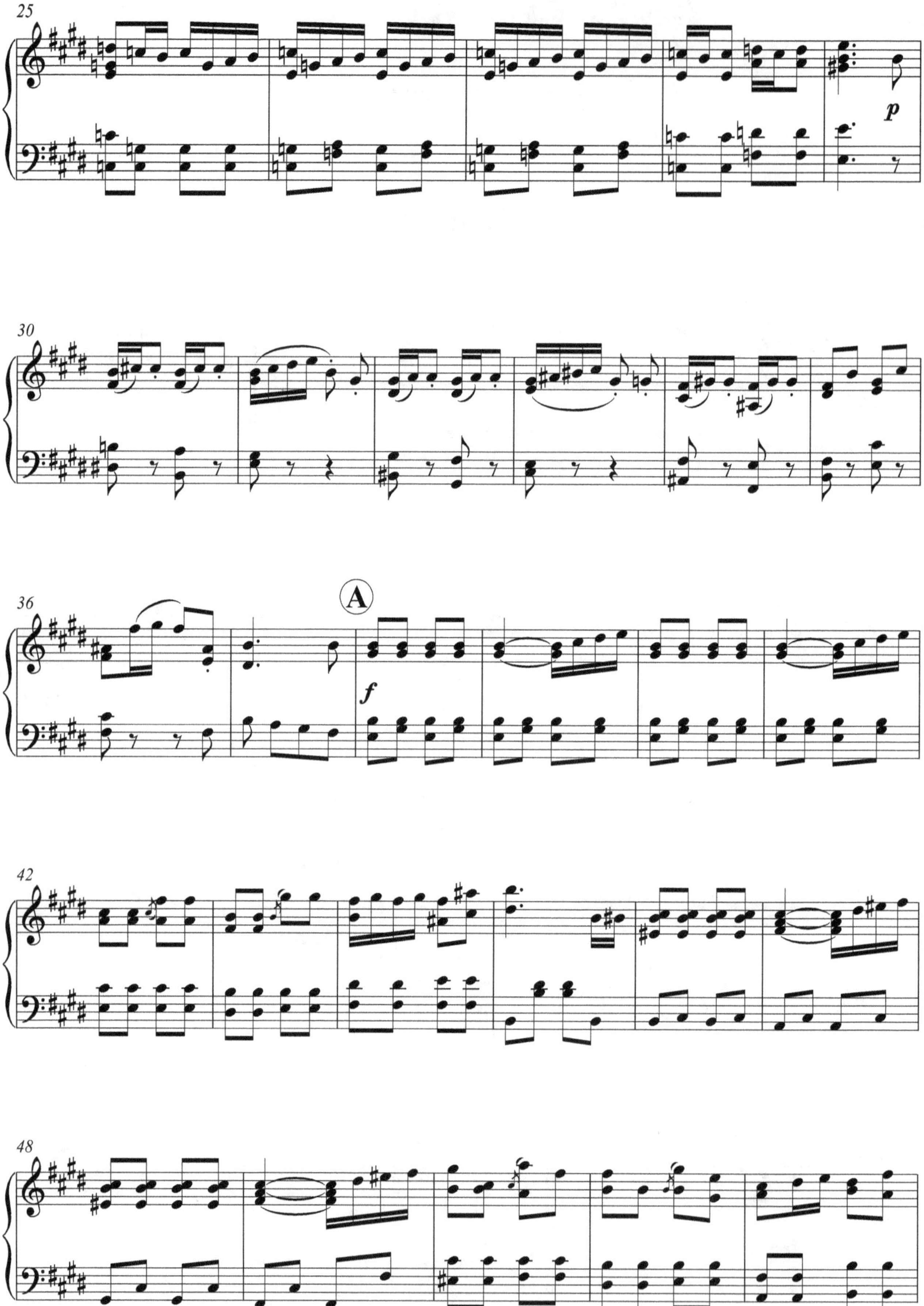
25
p
30
36
A
f
42
48

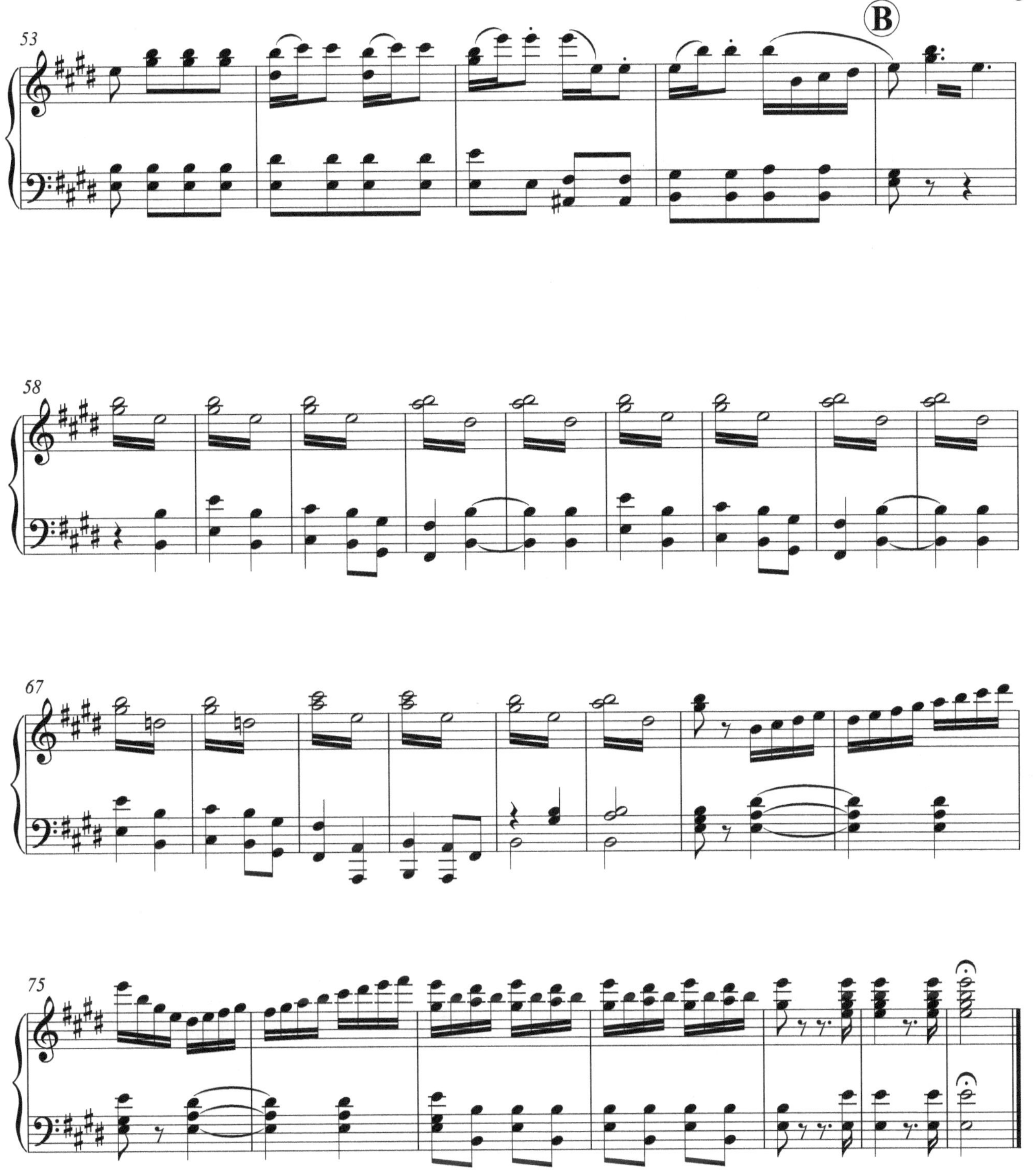
53
B
58
67
75

ACT I

SCENE.- The ruins of The Temple of the Gods on the summit of Mount Olympus. Picturesque shattered columns, overgrown with ivy, etc., R. and L., with entrances to temple (ruined) R. Fallen columns on the stage. Three broken pillars 2 R.E. At the back of stage is the approach to the summit of the mountain. This should be 'practicable' to enable large numbers of people to ascend and descend. In the distance are the summits of adjacent mountains. At first all this is concealed by a thick fog, which clears presently. Enter (through fog) Chorus of Stars coming off duty, as fatigued with their night's work.

No. I
CHORUS OF STARS, & SOLO SOPRANO
Throughout the Night

15
f
pp
21
CURTAIN
cresc
animé
29
(cresc)
ff
37
A
S&A.
pp
Through - out the night,
pp
43
S&A.
The con - stel - la - tions Have gi - ven light From var - ious sta - tions.

6

S&A. When mid - night gloom Falls on all nat-ions, We

T. *pp* (Bouche fermée) ou___ ou___

B. *pp* (Bouche fermée)

S&A. will re-sume our oc-cu - pa - tions.___ Through

T. ou___ ou___

S&A. out the night the con_ stel - la-tions have gi - ven light from var - ious sta - tions___

74
S&A.
When mid - night gloom Falls on all
T.
ou ou
B.
81
S&A.
nat-ions, We will re-sume our oc-cu-pa - tions.
B
88
Solo Star
Our light, it's true, Is not worth men - tion, What
8va

93

Solo Star: can we do to gain att - en - tion, When night and noon with vul - gar glar - ing, A

97

Solo Star: great big moon is *al -ways* flar - ing _____ When night and noon are

100

Solo Star: glar - ing, The_ moon is flar - ing?

C

105

S&A.: Through - out the night, The con - stel - la -tions Have gi - ven light

112
S&A.
T.
B.
From var-ious sta - tions.
(Bouche fermée)
ou
ou
(Bouche fermée)
When
119
S&A.
mid - night gloom Falls on all nat-ions, We will re-sume our oc-cu - pa - tions.
127
S&A.
dim a niente
We will re-sume our oc-cu - pa tions
dim
134
Exit chorus of stars
pp

During Chorus enter DIANA, *an elderly Goddess. She is carefully wrapped up in Cloaks, Shawls, etc. A hood is over her head, a respirator in her mouth, and galoshes on her feet. During the chorus she takes these things off, and discovers herself dressed in the usual costume of the Lunar Diana, the Goddess of the Moon*

Dia. (*shuddering*). Ugh! How cold the nights are! I don't know how it is, but I seem to feel the night air a great deal more than I used to. But it is time for the sun to be rising.

No. Ia
INSTRUMENTAL MUSIC
Diana's Hunting Call

Dia   (*after Apollo fails to make his entrance, calls*) Apollo!

Ap.   (*offstage tired and weary*) Hollo!

Dia   I've come off duty - it's time for you to be getting up.

    Enter APOLLO. *He is an elderly 'buck' with an air of assumed juvenility, and is dressed in dressing gown and smoking cap.*

Ap.   (*yawning*) I shan't go out today. I was out yesterday and the day before and I want a little rest

Dia.   My dear brother, I'm sure these short days can't hurt you. Why, you don't rise till six and you're in bed again by five: you should have a turn at my work and just see how you like that - out all night!

Ap.   My dear sister, I don't envy you - though I remember when I did - but that was when I was a younger sun. I don't think I'm quite well. Perhaps a little change of air will do me good. I've a great mind to show myself in London this Winter, they'll be very glad to see me. No! I shan't go out today. I shall send them this fine, thick, wholesome fog and they won't miss me. It's the best substitute for a blazing sun - and like most substitutes, nothing at all like the real thing. (*To fog*) Be off with you.

(Fog clears away and discovers the scene described).

No. Ib
INSTRUMENTAL MUSIC
Entrance of Mercury

MERCURY *shoots up from behind precipice at back of stage. He carries several parcels afterwards described. He sits down, very much fatigued.*

Mer   Home at last! And a nice time I've had of it.

Dia.   You young scamp you've been down all night again. This is the third time you've been out this week.

Mer.   Well you're a nice one to blow me up for that.

Dia.   I can't help being out all night.

Mer.   And I can't help being down all night. The very nature of Mercury requires that he should go down when the sun sets, and rise again, when the sun rises.

Dia.   And what have you been doing?

Mer.   Stealing on commission. There's a set of false teeth and a box of Vitamin Pills - that's for Jupiter . A toupee and a bottle of hair dye - that's for you Apollo . A respirator and a pair of galoshes - that's for Cupid – A full bottomed chignon , a bottle of peroxide, a box of face powder, a pot of rouge and a hare's foot, and that's all for Venus.

Dia.   Stealing! You ought to be ashamed of yourself!

Mer.   Oh, as the god of thieves I must do something to justify my position.

Dia. and Ap. (contemptuously). Your position!

Mer.   Oh I know it's nothing to boast of, even on earth. But up here, it's simply contemptible. Now that you gods are too old for your work, you've made me the miserable drudge of Olympus – groom, valet, postman, butler, commissionaire, maid of all work, parish beadle, and original dustman.

Ap.   Well your Christmas tips ought to be considerable.

Mer.   They ought to be, but they're not. I'm treated abominably. I make everybody and I'm nobody - I go everywhere and I'm nowhere - I do everything and I'm nothing. I've made thunder for Jupiter, written odes for Apollo, fought battles for Mars, and made love for Venus. I've married couples for Hymen, and six weeks after, I've divorced them for Cupid - and in return I get all the kicks while they pocket the tips. And in compensation for robbing me of the few ha'pennies in question, what have they done for me?

Ap.   Why they've - they've made you the god of thieves!

Mer.   How very self-denying of them - there isn't one of them who hasn't a better claim to the title than I have.

No. II
SONG (Mercury, with Diana & Apollo)
Oh, I'm the celestial drudge

Allegro moderato

Mercury

Diana

Apollo

Allegro moderato

ff   *p*

Merc.

Oh, I'm the ce - les - ti - al
I'm the slave of the gods, neck and
Then rea-ding and wri-ting I

drudge, From morn ing to night I must stop at it, On er-rands all day I must
heels, And I'm bound to o - bey, though I rate at 'em, And I not on - ly or-der their
teach, And spell-ing books ma - ny I've e - di - ted! And for bring-ing these arts with-in

Merc.

trudge, And I stick to my work 'till I drop at it! In sum-mer I get up at one, (As a
meals, But I cook 'em and serve 'em and wait at 'em. Then I make all their nec-tar-I do, (Which a
reach, That don-key Mi - ner - va gets cre-di-ted. Then I scrape at the stars with a knife, And plate

14

Merc.

good na-tured-don-key I'm ranked for it), Then I go and I light up the Sun, And
ter-ri-ble li-quor to rack us is), And when-e-ver I mix them a brew, Why
pow-der the moon(on the days for it), And I hear all the world and his wife A -

Merc.

Phoe-bus A-pol-lo gets thanked for it!
all the thanks-gi-vings are Bac-chus-'s!
war-ding Di-a-na the praise for it! Well,

Merc.

well, it's the way of the world, And will be through all it's fu-tur-i-ty, Though

Merc.

noo-dles are ba-roned and earled, There's no-thing for cle-ver ob-scu-ri-ty!

ff

31 3.

Merc.
ty! Well, well, it's the way of the world, And will be through all it's fu - tur - i - ty, Though

Di.
Well, well, it's the way of the world, And will be through all it's fu - tur - i - ty, Though

Ap.
Well, well, it's the way of the world, And will be through all it's fu - tur - i - ty, Though

36

Merc.
noo - dles are ba - roned and earled, There's no - thing for cle - ver ob - scu - ri -

Di.
noo - dles are ba - roned and earled, There's no - thing for cle - ver ob - scu - ri -

Ap.
noo - dles are ba - roned and earled, There's no - thing for cle - ver ob - scu - ri -

(After song – Thunder-Roll)

Ap   Why, who is this?

Dia. & Mer.   Jupiter!

All.   By Jove!

No. IIb
INSTRUMENTAL MUSIC
Entrance of Jupiter

Enter MARS *as Military Escort,he is very decrepit uses a walking stick and an ear- trumpet. He is followed by* JUPITER*, an extremely old man, with thin straggling white beard, he wears a long braided dressing-gown, handsomely trimmed, and a silk night-cap on his head.*

Jup.   At Ease Mars! Good day, Diana - ah, Apollo - Well, well, well, what's the matter? What's the matter?

Dia.   Why, that young scamp Mercury says that we do nothing, and leave all the duties of Olympus to him! Will you believe it , he's been putting it about that our influence on earth is dropping down to zero.

Jup.   Well, well - don't be hard on the lad - to tell you the truth, I'm not sure that he's very far wrong. Don't let it go any further, but between ourselves, the votive offerings have fallen off terribly of late. Why, I can remember the time when people offered us human sacrifices - no mistake about it - human sacrifices !

     Think of that !

Mars   Eh ,what ? (*using Ear Trumpe*t)

Jup.   Human Sacrifices!

Mars.   Ah! Those were the good old days .

Jup.   Then it fell off to oxen, pigs, and sheep.

Ap.   Well, there are worse things than oxen, pigs, and sheep.

Jup.   So I've found to my cost. My dear Sir - between ourselves, it's dropped off from one thing to another until it has positively dwindled down to tins of preserved Australian Beef! What do you think of that?

Mars.   Eh ? What ?

Jup   Australian Beef! (*shouting down Ear Trumpet*).

Mars.   No thank- ye, I've already dined .

     (Mercury *returns in great anxiety and tries to get Jupiter's attention*).

Jup.   You won't mention it - it might go further -In short, matters have come to such a crisis that there's no mistake about it - something must be done to restore our influence, the only question is, What?

Mars   (*Using Ear Trumpet*)   What?

Jup.   (*Shouting at* Mercury)   WHAT!

No. III

QUINTET (Mercury, Diana, Mars, Apollo & Jupiter).

Oh incident unprecedented

Allegro moderato

Mercury: Oh in - ci - dent un - pre - ce - den - ted! I

Diana:

Mars:

Apollo:

Jupiter:

Allegro moderato

f *p*

Merc.: har - dly can be - lieve it's true!_

Mars: Why bless the boy he's quite de - men - ted! Why, what's the mat - ter,

11
A
Merc.
Mars
Ap.
Why mor - tals up the
sir, with you?
Speak quick - ly or you'll get a war - ming!
f
p
15
Merc.
mount are swar - ming, Our tem - ple on Ol - ym - pus storm - ing, In
18
Merc.
hun - dreds, aye, in ma - ny thou - sands, too!

20

Merc./Di./Mars/Ap./Jup. (m. 21): Good - ness gra - cious, How au - da - cious! Earth is spa - cious, Why come here?

Merc./Di./Mars/Ap./Jup. (m. 25): Our im - pe - ding Their pro - ceed - ing Were good breed - ing, That is ve - ry

29
C
Merc.
clear! How au - da - cious Why come here?
Di.
Good ness gra - cious! Earth is spa - cious! Oh good - ness gra - cious why come
Mars
Good-ness gra - cious! Earth is spa - cious! Oh good - ness gra - cious why come
Ap.
How au - da - cious Why come here? Why come
Jup.
How au - da - cious Why come here? Why come
f
p
f
p

33
Merc.
How au - da - cious Why come here?
Di.
here? Good ness gra - cious! Earth is spa - cious! Oh good - ness gra - cious why come
Mars
here? Good-ness gra - cious! Earth is spa - cious! Oh good - ness gra - cious why come
Ap.
here? How au - da - cious Why come here? Why come
Jup.
here? How au - da - cious Why come here? Why come
f
p
f
p

37 Poco accel

Merc. Good-ness gra-cious! How au-da-cious! Good-ness gra-cious! How au-da-cious!

Di. here? Good-ness gra-cious! How au-da-cious! Good-ness gra-cious!

Mars here? Good-ness gra-cious! How au-da-cious! Good-ness gra-cious! How au-da-cious!

Ap. here? Good-ness gra-cious! How au-da-cious! Good-ness gra-cious!

Jup. here? Good-ness gra-cious! How au-da-cious! Good-ness gra-cious!

Poco accel

41 Accelerando *cresc*

Merc. Good-ness gra-cious! How au-da-cious Earth is spa-cious why, oh why come

Di. *cresc* Good-ness gra-cious! How au-da-cious Earth is spa-cious why, oh why come

Mars *cresc* Good-ness gra-cious! How au-da-cious Earth is spa-cious why, of why come

Ap. *cresc* Good-ness gra-cious! How au-da-cious Earth is spa-cious why, oh why come

Jup. *cresc* Good-ness gra-cious! How au-da-cious Earth is spa-cious why, oh why come

Accelerando

p *cresc*

Allegretto agitato
45
Merc.
here?
Di.
here?
Oh
Mars
here?
Ap.
here?
Jup.
here?
Allegretto agitato
8va
f
mp
p
49
D
Di.
Ju - pi - ter hear my plea, Up - on the mount if they light, There'll
53
Di.
be an end of me, I won't be seen by day-light

Ap. Tar-ta-rus is the place These scoun-drels you_____ should send to: Should

Ap. they be-hold my face My in-flu-ence there's_____ an

Merc. Should they be-hold his face, His in-flu-ence there's____ an end to!

Di. Should they be-hold his face, His in-flu-ence there's____ an end to!

Mars Should they be-hold his face, His in-flu-ence there's____ an end to!

Ap. end to!

Jup. What

fools they are to give them selves so much_____ ex - er - tion.

A

gov - ern-ment sur - vey, up here I'll make_____ as - ser - tion!

Or could it be the Al - pine Club at

It looks to me more like a Thom - as Cook's____ ex - cur - sion!

their_____ di - ver - sion!

F
85
♩.=♩ Allegro moderato come prima
Merc.
Di.
Mars
Ap.
Jup.
Ah, Good-ness gra-cious, How au-da-cious! Earth is spa-cious, Why come here?
Ah, Good-ness gra-cious, How au-da-cious! Earth is spa-cious, Why come here?
Ah, Good-ness gra-cious, How au-da-cious! Earth is spa-cious, Why come here?
Ah, Good-ness gra-cious, How au-da-cious! Earth is spa-cious, Why come here?
Ah, Good-ness gra-cious, How au-da-cious! Earth is spa-cious, Why come here?
♩.=♩ Allegro moderato come prima
90
Merc.
Di.
Mars
Ap.
Jup.
Our im-pe-ding Their pro-ceed-ing Were good breed-ing, That is ve-ry
Our im-pe-ding Their pro-ceed-ing Were good breed-ing, That is ve-ry
Our im-pe-ding Their pro-ceed-ing Were good breed-ing, That is ve-ry
Our im-pe-ding Their pro-ceed-ing Were good breed-ing, That is ve-ry
Our im-pe-ding Their pro-ceed-ing Were good breed-ing, That is ve-ry

94
Merc.
Di.
Mars
Ap.
Jup.
Clear
Clear
Clear
Clear
Clear
mf
md
p
100
G
Ap.
If, migh - ty Jove, you val - ue you ex - is - tence, Send them a thun - der
106
Ap.
bolt with your re gards!
Jup.
My thun - der - bolts, though va - lid at a dis - tance,

112
Merc.
Jup.
Let the moon's rays, Di-a - na,
Are not ef-fec - tive at a hun - dred yards.
md
118
Merc.
strike - 'em fligh - ty, Make them all lun - a-tics in var - ious styles
124
Di.
My Lu - nar rays un - hap - pi - ly are migh - ty
128
Di.
On - ly at a hun - dred thou - sand miles.

132
H
Merc.
Di.
Mars
Ap.
Jup.
Ah, Good-ness gra-cious, How au-da-cious! Earth is spa-cious, Why come here?

137
Merc.
Di.
Mars
Ap.
Jup.
Our im-pe-ding Their pro-ceed-ing Were good breed-ing, That is ve-ry

141
I
Merc.
Di.
Mars
Ap.
Jup.
clear! How au - da - cious Why come here?
clear! Good ness gra - cious! Earth is spa - cious! Oh good - ness gra - cious why come
clear! Good-ness gra - cious! Earth is spa - cious! Oh good - ness gra - cious why come
clear! How au - da - cious Why come here? why come
clear! How au - da - cious Why come here? why come
f p f p
145
Merc.
Di.
Mars
Ap.
Jup.
How au - da - cious Why come here?
here? Good ness gra - cious! Earth is spa - cious! Oh good - ness gra - cious why come
here? Good-ness gra - cious! Earth is spa - cious! Oh good - ness gra - cious why come
here? How au - da - cious Why come here? Why come
here? How au - da - cious Why come here? Why come
f p f p

(Hurried Exeunt JUPITER, APOLLO, DIANA, MARS, and MERCURY into ruined temple).

Enter SPARKEION *and* NICEMIS *climbing mountain at back.*

Spark. Here we are at last on the very summit, and we've left the others ever so far behind! Why, what's this?

Nice. A ruined palace! A palace on the top of a mountain? I wonder who lives here? Some mighty king, I dare say, with wealth beyond all counting, who came to live up here …

Spark. To avoid his creditors! It's a lovely situation for a country house, though it's very much out of repair.

Nice. Its a very in-convenient situation.

Spark. In-convenient?

Nice. Yes - how are you to get butter, milk, and eggs up here? No pigs - no poultry and no postman. Why, I should go mad.

Spark. What a dear little practical mind you have! What a wife you will make!

Nice. Don't be too sure - we are only partly married you know – and the marriage ceremony lasts all day.

Spark. I've no doubt about it at all. We shall be as happy as a King and Queen, though we are only a strolling actor and actress.

Nice. It's very kind of Thespis to celebrate our marriage day by giving the company a pic-nic on this lovely mountain.

Spark. And still more kind of him to allow us to get so much ahead of all the others - discreet Thespis! (*kissing her*).

Nice. There now, get away, do! Remember the marriage ceremony is not yet completed.

Spark. But it would be ungrateful to Thespis's discretion not to take advantage of it by improving the opportunity.

Nice. Certainly not; get away.

Spark. On second thoughts the opportunity's so good it don't admit of improvement. There! (*kisses her*).

Nice. How dare you kiss me before we are quite married!

Spark. Attribute it to the intoxicating influence of the mountain air.

Nice. Then we had better go down again. It is not right to expose ourselves to influences over which we have no control.

No. IV
DUET (Nicemis & Sparkeion)
Here far away

Here far a-way from all the world, Dis - sen-sion and de-ri - sion, With Na-ture's won-ders all un-furled To our de - li-ghted vi - sion, With

Sp. no - one here (at least in sight) To in - ter - fere with our de - light, And

Sp. two fond lo - vers se - ver, Oh do not free thine hand from mine, I

Sp. swear to thee My love is thine, For e - ver and for - e - ver!

Nic. On

B

33 Nic. moun-tain top the air is keen, And most ex-hil-ar - a - ting, And

legato

37 Nic. we say things we do not mean, In mo-ments less e - la - ting. So

poco più detaché

41 Nic. please to wait for thoughts that crop, En *tête à tête* on mountain top, May

45 Nic. not ex-act-ly ta - ly With those that you may en - ter tain, Re -

Nic. *tur-ning to the so-ber plain Of yon re-lax-ing val - ley. You*

Nic. *swear your love is mine for e - ver and for-e -*

Sp. *I swear my love is thine for e - ver and for-e -*

Colla voce

Nic. *ver! For - e - ver, For e -*

Sp. *ver! For - e - ver, For e -*

Colla voce

Spark.	Very well - if you won't have anything to say to me, I know who will.
Nice.	Who will?
Spark.	Daphne will.
Nice.	Daphne would flirt with anybody.
Spark.	Anybody would flirt with Daphne. She is quite as pretty as you , she has appreciation and she likes good looks.
Nice.	We all like what we haven't got!
Spark.	She keeps her eyes open.
Nice.	Yes – One of them.
Spark.	Which one?
Nice.	The one she doesn't wink with.
Spark.	Well, I was engaged to her for six months and if she still makes eyes at me, you must attribute it to force of habit. Besides - remember - we are only half-married at present.
Nice.	Then I suppose you mean that you are going to treat me as shamefully as you treated her. Very well, break it off if you like. I shall not offer any objection. *(cue music)* Thespis used to be very attentive to me, and I'd just as soon be a manager's wife as a fifth-rate actor's!
Spark .	Fifth rate actor! How dare you call me a fith rate actor, you…sixth rate soubrette!

38

Chorus heard, at first below, then enter DAPHNE, PRETTEIA, SILLIMON, TIPSEION, CYMON, and other members of THESPIS' company climbing over rocks at back. All carry items for the pic-nic.

No. V
CHORUS OF MORTALS & SOLOS (Soprano, Alto, Tenor & Bass)
Climbing over rocky mountain

21
A
Mortals
Climb-ing o - ver__ rock-y moun-tain, Skip-ping riv - u - let and foun-tain,
25
wil - lows qui - - - ver
Mortals
Pass-ing where the__ wil-lows qui-ver, By the e - ver rol - ling ri - ver,
29
Mortals
Pass - ing where the__ wil - lows qui - ver By the e - ver rol - ling ri - ver,

Swol - len with the sum - mer rain the sum - mer rain.

Thread - ing long and leaf - y ma - zes, Dot - ted with un - num-bered dai - sies,

Dot - ted dot - ted with un - num - bered dai - - - sies,

45
Mortals
Sca - ling rough and__ rug - ged pass - es, Climb the har - dy lads and las - ses,
49
Mortals
'Till the moun - tain top, The moun - tain top they gain.
53
Mortals
Sca - ling rough and rug - ged pass - es, Climb the har - dy lads and lass - es,

Mortals: 'Till the moun - tain top they gain.

Ten.: Fill the cup and tread the mea - sure,

Make the most of fleet - ing___ lei - sure, Hail it as a

true al - ly, Though it per - ish___ bye and

bye!

Hail it as a true al - ly, Though it per -ish bye and bye!

Ev - 'ry mo - ment brings a___ trea___ sure Of it's own es -

44

Sop. -pe - cial__ plea - sure; Though the mo - ments quick - ly die,

Sop. Greet them gai - ly__ as they fly! Greet them gai - ly__ as they

Sop. fly!

Mortals Though the mo - ments quic - kly die, Greet them gai - ly as they

114
Mortals
fly!
119
D
Bass
Far a - way from grief and care, High up in the
p
125
Bass
moun - tain air, Let us live and reign a -
130
Bass
lone In a world that's all our own.

135
Alto
Here en - thro - néd in the sky, Far a - way from mor - tal
142
Alto
eye, We'll be gods and make de - crees, They may hon - our_ them who
149
Alto
please.
Mortals
We'll be gods and make de - crees_ They may hon - our them who please.
f
ff
154
sf

Mortals: Fill the cup and tread the mea - sure,

Mortals: Make the most of fleet - ing lei - sure,

Mortals: Hail it as a true al - ly, Though it per - ish

175

Mortals bye and bye! Hail it as a true al - ly,

181

F

Mortals Though it per - ish bye and bye! Fill the cup and

186

Mortals tread the mea-sure, Make the most of fleet-ing lei - sure, Hail it as a true al - ly a

After CHORUS AND COUPLETS, *enter* THESPIS *climbing over rocks.*

Thes.   Bless you, my people, bless you. Let the revels commence! After all, for thorough, unconstrained, un-conventional enjoyment give me a pic-nic.

Sill.   A pic-nic ! No-body mentioned a pic-nic to me , it wasn't in the company call-sheet.

Thes.   Be quiet Sillimon - don't interrupt.

Sill.   Ha! shut up again! Typical, the Stage Manager is always the last to be told.

Thes.   Now the best of a pic-nic is that everybody contributes what he pleases, and nobody knows what anybody else has brought till the last moment. Now, unpack everybody and let's see what there is.

Nice.   I have brought you - a bottle of soda water - for the claret-cup.

Daph.   I have brought you - a lettuce and a hard boiled egg for the lobster salad.

Prett.   A bunch of burrage for the claret cup.

Spark.   A bottle of vinegar - for the lobster salad.

Timid.   One lump of sugar - for the claret cup.

Sill.   He has brought one lump of sugar for the claret-cup! Ha !

Thes.   Well, Sillimon, and what have you brought?

Sill.	Let me see (*searching in his pockets*) well I have…a barley sugar ….and a peppermint drop for ….the …. claret cup.
Thes.	Oh - is that all?
Sill.	All! Ha! He asks if that is all! (*as one used to being under–appreciated*).
Thes.	But, I say - this is capital so far as it goes - nothing could be better, but it doesn't go far enough. The claret cup, for instance I don't insist on claret . Or the lobster -I don't insist on lobster, but a lobster salad without any lobster, why - it isn't lobster salad. Here Tipseion!

Tipseion *(a very drunken bloated fellow, dressed, however ,with scrupulous accuracy and wearing a large medal round his neck).* My master!

(Falls on his knees to THESPIS *and kisses his coat)*

Thes.	Get up - don't be a fool.(*aside*) Where's the claret? We arranged last week that you were to see to that?
Tips.	True, dear master. But then I was a drunkard!
Thes.	You were.
Tips.	You engaged me to play "convivial" parts on the strength of my personal appearance.
Thes.	I did.
Tips.	You then found out that my " habits " interfered with my duties as low comedian.
Thes.	True -
Tips.	You said yesterday that unless I took the pledge, you would dismiss me from your Company.
Thes.	Quite so.
Tips.	Good. I have taken it. It is all I have taken since yesterday. My preserver! (*tries to embrace him*).
Thes.	Yes, that's all very well, but where's the wine?
Tips.	Oh, I left it behind, that I might not be tempted to violate my pledge.
Thes.	Oh! Minion! Ye are odious to my sight! Get out of it!
	Well let's try and enjoy ourselves. Ha! ha! (*the rest of the company laugh half-heartedly*) It is well for those who can laugh - let them do so - there is no extra charge. The light-hearted cup and the convivial jest for them - but for me - what is there for me?
Sill.	There is some claret cup and lobster salad. (*handing him some*).
Thes.	Thank you. (*resuming his soliloquy*) What is there for me but anxiety-ceaseless, gnawing anxiety that tears at my very vitals and rends my peace of mind asunder! The charge of these thoughtless revellers is my unhappy lot. It is not a small charge, and it is rightly termed "a lot", because there are many. Oh why did the Gods make me a manager?

Spark.	*(as guessing a riddle) Why* did the gods make him a manager?
Daph.	Why did the *gods* make him a manager?
Sill.	Why did the gods make *him* a manager?
Prett.	Why did the gods make him a *manager*?
Thes.	No – no- What are you all talking about? What do you mean?
Daph.	I've got it - don't tell us -
All.	*(Everyone arguing and talking together)* No - no – its because –because-
Thes.	*(annoyed)* STOP! It isn't a conundrum! It's a misanthropical question. Why cannot I join you ?

(THESPIS retires up centre).

Daph.	*(who is sitting with* SPARKEION *to the annoyance of* NICEMIS, *who is crying alone)* I'm sure I don't know. We do not want you. Don't distress yourself on our account - we are getting on very comfortably - aren't we, Sparkeion?
Spark.	We are so happy that we don't miss the lobster or the claret. What are lobster and claret compared with the society of those we love?
Daph	Why Nicemis, love, you are eating nothing. Aren't you happy dear?
Nice	*(Spitefully).* You are quite welcome to my share of everything. I intend to console myself with the society of my Manager.

(Takes THESPIS' *arm affectionately).*

Thes.	Here I say - this won't do, you know - I can't allow it - well, at least not before the company. Besides, you are half- married to Sparkeion. Sparkeion, here's your half-wife impairing my influence before the company. Don't you know the story of the gentleman who undermined his influence by associating with his inferiors?
All.	Yes – Yes - we know it. *(desperate not to hear the song again).*
Sill.	I do not know it! T'was ever thus! Doomed to disappointment from my earliest years .
Thes.	There - there that's enough Sillimon - you shall hear it.

No. VI
SONG (Thespis & Chorus)
I once knew a chap

Allegro moderato

Thespis

Chorus of Mortals

Allegro moderato

f

5

Th.

I

mf

11 Ⓐ

Th.

once knew a chap who dis charged a fun-ction on the North South East West Did-dle-sex jun-ction,

p sim

sim

He was con-spic-u -ous ex-ceed-ing for his aff-a-ble ways and his ea-sy breed-ing. Al-

though a chair-man of Di-rec-tors, He was hand in glove with the ti-cket in-spec-tors, He

tipped the guards with brand new fi-vers And sang lit-tle songs to the en-gine dri-vers.

B

Each Christ-mas Day he gave each sto-ker A sil-ver sho-vel and a gol den po-ker, He'd but-ton hole flowers for the tick - et sort-ers, And rich bath buns for the out-side port-ers. He'd

mount the clerks on his first class hun-ters, And he built lit -tle vil-las for the road side shun-ters, And if

a -ny were fond of___ pi -geon shoot ing, He'd ask them down to his place at Toot- ing.

'Twas

Th. *(49)* told to me with great com-punc-tion, By one who had dis-charged with unc-tion, A

Th. *(53)* Chair-man of Di - rec - tors func-tion on the North South East West Did-dle-sex Junc-tion

Chorus 'Twas

Chorus *(57)* told to him with great com-punc-tion, By one who had dis-charged with unc-tion, A

Chorus: Chair-man of Di - rec - tors fun-ction on the North South East West Did-dle-sex Jun-ction

Chorus: Fol did - dle, lol - did - dle, lol, Fol lol lol Lol lol lay!

Th. In

Chorus: Fol did-dle, lol did-dle, lol lol lay. Fol did-dle, lol did-dle, lol lol lay.

course of time there spread a rum-our That he did all this from a sense of hum-our, So in-

stead of sig-nal-ling and sto-king, They gave them-selves up to a course of jo-king. When

e-ver they knew that he was ri-ding, They shun-ted his train on a lone-ly si-ding, Or

stopped all night in the mid-dle of a tun nel, On the plea that the boi-ler was a-com-ing through the fun nel.

58

If he wished to go to___ Perth or Stir-ling, His train through sev-er-al coun-ties___whirl-ing, Would set him down in a fit of lar-king, At four a. m. in the wilds of bark-ing. This pleased his whim and___ seemed to strike it, But the gen-e-ral pub-lic did not like it, The re-ceipts fell, a-fter a few re-peat-ings, And he got it hot at the an-nual meet-ings.

107
Th.
'Twas
111
E
Th.
told to me with great com-punc-tion, By one who had dis-charged with un-ction, A
115
Th.
Chair-man of Di - rec - tors fun-ction on the North South East West Did-dle-sex Jun-ction
Chorus
'Twas

119 Chorus: told to him with great com-punc-tion, By one who had dis-charged with un-ction, A

123 Chorus: Chair-man of Di-rec-tors fun-ction on the North South East West Did-dle-sex Jun-ction

127 Chorus: Fol did-dle, lol-did-dle, lol, Fol lol lol Lol lol lay!

131 **Slower**   Ⓕ

He fol-lowed out his whim with vi-gour, The shares went down to a no-mi-nal fi-gure.

137

These are the sad re-sults pro-ceed-ing, From his af-fa-ble ways and his ea-sy breed-ing! The

141

line, with it's rails and guards and peel-ers, Was sold for a song to ma-rine-store deal-ers, The

145   **A tempo - Allegro moderato**

share hol-ders are all in the work' uss, And he sells pipe lights in the Re-gent Cir-cus.

62

'Twas told to me with great com-punc-tion, By one who had dis-

charged with un-ction, A Chair-man of Di - rec - tors fun-ction on the North South East West

Did-dle-sex Jun-ction

'Twas told to him with great com-punc-tion, By one who had dis- charged with un ction, A

Chair-man of Di - rec - tors fun-ction on the North South East West Did-dle-sex Jun-ction

Fol did - dle, lol did - dle, lol, Fol lol lol Lol lol lay!

Fol did - dle, lol - did - dle lol, Fol lol lol Lol lol lay!

Thes   Still I am not happy. As a man I am naturally of an easy disposition.As a Manager, I am compelled to hold myself aloof, so that my influence may not be deteriorated. As a man, I am inclined to fraternise with the pauper - as a Manager I am compelled to walk about like this: Don't know yah! Don't know yah! Don't know yah!

(Strides haughtily about the stage.(THUNDERCLAP) JUPITER, MARS, and APOLLO, in full Olympian costume appear on the three broken columns. Thespians scream.)

Jup., Mars and Ap. Presumptuous mortals!

Thes   *(same business)* Don't know yah! Don't know yah!

Jup., Mars and Ap. *(seated on three broken pillars)* Presumptuous mortals!

Thes.   I do not know you. - I do not know you.

Jup., Mars and Ap.   *(standing on ground)* Presumptuous mortal!

Thes.   Remove these persons.

Jup.   Stop, you evidently *don't* know me. Allow me to offer you my card.

(Throws flash paper)

Thes.   Ah Yes, it's very pretty, but we don't want any of that sort of thing at present. When we next do our Christmas Burlesque, I'll let you know. *(Changing his manner)* Look here, this is a private party you know and you haven't been invited. There are a good many other mountains about, if you must have a mountain all to yourself. Don't make me let myself down before my company. *(Resuming)* Don't know yah! Don't know yah!

Jup.   Presumptous mortal, I am Jupiter, the King of the Gods. This is Apollo and this is Mars.

(All mortals kneel to them except THESPIS*)*.

Thes.   Oh! Then as I'm a respectable man, and rather particular about the company I keep, I think I'll go ...

Mars.   What do you mean by that Sir!

Thes.   Why, the scandalous behaviour of some of the gods is perfectly common knowledge. And if you think we don't know about those shocking affairs with Danae - and Leda - and Europa, you're very much mistaken. Good-Bye! *(about to go)*.

Jup.   No - no - stop a bit, Come back. We want to consult you on a matter of great importance.

Thes.   Well- I suppose I can give you five minutes.

Jup.   No matter. It will suffice.

Thes.   *(to Thespians)* Ladies and Gentlemen of the Company I have been invited to confer with a brother manager. As our discussion is not for the ears of the *oi polloi*, I should be very much obliged if you would all withdraw to a respectable distance.

(They are reluctant to go).

Jup.   *(steps forward).* Allow me -

Throws thunderbolt. Flashpot effect and Roll on Thundersheet Thespians scream in terror and exeunt.

Jup.   Now , who are you Sir ?

Thes.   I am Thespis, Sole -Proprietor, Manager and Licensee of the Thessalian The-a-tres. *(offers card).*

Jup.   Ah! The very man we want. Now as a judge of what the public likes, are you   impressed with my appearance as father of the gods?

Thes.   Well to be candid with you, I am not. In fact, I'm disappointed.

Jup.   Disappointed?

Thes.   Yes, you see you're so much out of repair. No, you don't come up to my idea of the part and bless you, I've played you often.

Jup.   You have!

Thes.   To be sure I have.

Jup.   And how have you dressed for the part?

Thes.   Fine commanding party in the prime of life. Thunderbolts - full beard - dignified manner - a good deal of this sort of thing ' Don't know yah! Don't know yah !' Oh it's very effective you know especially ,Ha Ha, up in…..THE GODS !   Ha !

Jup.   *(much affected).* Hmm - I'm very much obliged to you. It's very good of you. I –I used to be like that. I can't tell you how much I feel it. But do you find I'm still an impressive character to play?

Thes.   Well…. No! I can't say you are. In fact we don't use you much out of …The Burlesque!

Jup.   The Burlesque! *(shocked)*

Thes.   Yes, it's a painful subject, drop it, drop it. Look, the fact is, you are not the gods you were - you're behind the times.

App.   Well, but what are we to do? We feel that we ought to do something, but we don't know what.

Enter DIANA *(* or VENUS *) veiled during the following speech*

Thes.   Well If you really wish to know at first hand the public opinion of the gods why not accept a starring engagement with my Company and tour the Thessalian provinces.You'll soon find out what the public thinks of you. Especially if you play Sparta on a wet Monday night. Yes I can see it now "The h'Original Gods every night in Burlesque" what a heading for a six-sheet poster.

Jup.   I'm sure that's a very good idea, but you see, we're all a little past it don't you think

Dia.(or Venus)   *(offended)* I am not past it. I would love to appear in a burlesque.

Thes.   I'm afraid I haven't had the pleasure. Introduce us somebody.

Jup. Diana *(Venus)*, this is Mr. Thespis of the Thessalian The-a-tres. Mr. Thespis, this is the Godess Diana. *(Venus)*

Thes Charmed Madam

Dia. (or Venus) - (raising her veil) Miss!

Thes. . *(somewhat disappointed).* Oh! a veiled surprise! Look, why don't you all go down to earth incognito, mingle with the world, hear and see what people think of you, and judge for yourselves as to the best means to take to restore your influence?

Ap. Ah, but what's to become of Olympus in the meantime?

Thes. Lor bless you, don't distress yourself about that. I've a very good company, used to taking long parts on the shortest notice. Invest us with your powers and we'll fill your places till you return.

Jup. *(aside)* Hmm, The offer's tempting. But suppose you fail?

Thes. Fail! Fail! Oh, we never fail in our profession. We've nothing but great successes!

Jup. Very well. In order that you may not be entirely without assistance we will leave you Mercury and whenever you find yourself in a difficulty you can consult him. Now take heed Mr Thespis If you succeed, you may return to earth with such gifts as only the gods can bestow upon you. But if you fail, you will be constituted "Father of the Drama" and be held accountable for everything that every author may write in ages to come.

Thes. Oh I say - that's a terrible responsibility when you think of some of the rubbish they put on in London these days! *(thinks about it)* Well- never let it be said that I refused to assist a brother manager in distress.

Jup. Then it's a bargain?

Thes. It's a bargain.

(They shake hands on it)

No. VII
FINALE ACT I
(Mercury, Diana, Apollo, Jupiter, Thespis, Nicemis, Daphne, Sparkeion, Timidon & Chorus of Gods and Mortals)

Jup. that's ar-ranged-you take my place, my boy, While we make tri - al of a new ex-

Jup. is - tence At length I shall be a - ble to en - joy the plea-sures I have en - vied from a

Merc. Com - pelled u-pon Ol-y - mpus here to stop, While

Jup. di - stance.

Merc. o - ther gods go down to play the he - ro, Don't be sur-prised if on this moun-tain

Merc. top, You find your Mer-cur-y is down at ze - ro!

Ap. To earth a-way! to join in mor-tal acts, And

Ap. ga-ther fresh ma-ter - i-al to write on, In ves-ti-gate more close-ly sev-'ral

Di. / Ap. facts, That I for cen-tu-ries have thrown some light on! I,

33
Di.
as the mo - dest moon with cre - scent bow, Have al - ways shown a light to night - ly
36
Di.
scan - dal, I must say I should like to go be - low, And find out
39
Di.
if the game is worth the can - dle!
f
B Poco più mosso e energico
43
ff
mf

* (Enter all the Thespians, summoned by MERCURY) *

MERCURY (over orchestra): "Here come your people"   THESPIS (over orchestra) "Better people now!"

(♩≈♩.) **Meno mosso, allegretto**

Th.

While migh - ty Jove goes down be - low with

all the o - ther de - i - ties, I fill his place and wear his clo', The ve - ry part for

me it is. To mo - ther earth to make a track they all are spurred and boot - ed too, And

you will fill, 'till they come back the parts you best are suit - ed to. And

you will fill 'till they come back the parts you best are suit - ed to. Ah

77
Th.
Ah
The parts you best are suit-ed to.
mf
The
Chorus of Mortals
Ah
Ah
The
mf
Ah
Ah
mf
83
Th.
parts you best are suit - ed to, Are suit - - - ed to.
Chorus of Mortals
parts we best are suit - ed to, Are suit - - - ted to.
Più mosso
Più mosso
f
88
ff

D
93
mf
Chorus of Gods and Mortals
Here's a pret - ty tale for fu - ture Il - i - ads and Od - y- sseys;
mf
mf
97
Chorus of Gods and Mortals
Mor - tals are a - bout_ to per - son - ate the gods and god-des- ses.
101
Chorus of Gods and Mortals
Now to set the world in or - der, we will work in un - i - ty, For

105
Chorus of Gods and Mortals
f
Ju - pi - ter's per - plex - i - ty is Thes pi - s' op - por - tu - ni - ty. Now to
109
Chorus of Gods and Mortals
set the world in or - der, We will work in per - fect u - ni - ty, For
113
Chorus of Gods and Mortals
Ju - pi - ter's per - plex - i - ty is Thes-pis-s' Op - por - tu - ni - ty.

Poch accel

$\sharp = \flat$ **Allegro grazioso**

Nic.

2nd Verse

Ⓔ

am the moon the lamp of night. I show a light, I show a light. With

Sp.

1st Verse

Phoe - bus am I with gol - den ray, the God of Day, the God of Day, When

Tim.

3rd Verse

Migh-ty Mars, the God of War, I'm des-tined for I'm des-tined for, A

p

140

Nic. *ra-di-ant sheen I put to flight The sha-dows of the sky.* By

Sp. *shad-o-wy night has held her sway, I make the god-dess fly.* 'Tis

Tim. *ter-ri-bly fa-mous con-que-ror, With sword up-on his thigh.* When

144 **Poco meno e poch colla voce**

Nic. *my fair rays, as you're a-ware, Gay lo-vers swear, gay lo-vers swear, While*

Sp. *mine the task to wake the world, In slum-ber curled in slum-ber curled; By*

Tim. *ar-mies meet with ea-ger shout, And war-like rout, and war-like rout, You'll*

148 **quasi tempo e poch accel**

Nic. *grey-beards sleep a-way their care, The lamp of night am*

Sp. *me her charms are all un-furled, The God of Day am*

Tim. *find me there with-out a doubt. The God of War am*

151
In tempo
Nic.
I!
Sp.
I!
Tim.
I!
mf
Chorus of Gods and Mortals
The God of Day, Yes, that part shall our Spark-eion
The lamp of night, Our Nice-mis plays to her de-
The God of War, Great Tim-i-don is des-tined
mf
The God of Day,
The lamp of night,
The God of War,
In tempo
mf
155
Chorus of Gods and Mortals
play. Ha ha ha ha ha ha ha ha! Yes that part shall our Spark-eion
light, Ha ha ha ha ha ha ha ha! Our Nice-mis plays to her de-
for! Ha ha ha ha ha ha ha ha! Great Tim-i-don is des-tined

159
F
Chorus of Gods and Mortals
play!
light!
for!
The rar-est fun and rar-est fare that e-ver fell to mor-tal share. Ha
165
Nic.
1.2.
I
Chorus of Gods and Mortals
ha ha ha ha ha! The rar-est fun and fare.
1.2.
173
3. Slower
Daph.
When, as the fruit of war-like deeds, The sol-dier bleeds the sol-dier bleeds, Cal-

178
Daph.
li - o - pe crowns her - o - ic deeds, With im - mor - tal - i - ty. I
182
Daph.
A tempo
glor - i - fy the sol - dier's name, And write it on the roll of fame Yes, yes the Muse of Fame am
188
Daph.
I!
Chorus of Gods and Mortals
Yes, yes the muse of fame is she! Ha ha ha ha ho ho ho ho! The

Muse of Fame, The Muse of Fame, Cal - li - o - pe is Daph -ne's name, Cal -

li - o - pe, Cal - li - o - pe is Daph - ne's name. Ha ha ha ha ha! ha! ha!

82

Allegro risoluto

H With mortal principals

Chorus of Mortals

Here's a pret-ty tale for fu-ture Il - i - ads and Od-y-sseys;

Chorus of Mortals

Mor-tals are a-bout to per-son-ate the gods and god-des-ses.

232
Chorus of Mortals
Now to set the world in order, we will work in un - i - ty, For
236
Chorus of Mortals
Ju - pi - ter's per - plex - i - ty is Thes-pis-'s op - por - tu - ni - ty.
240
With principal deities
p
Chorus of Gods
We will go down be - low, down be - low, down be - low,
p
p

244
Chorus of Gods
Chorus of Mortals
Re - vels_ rare,_ We will share, What re - vels we will share. Ha ha ha
Ha ha ha
f

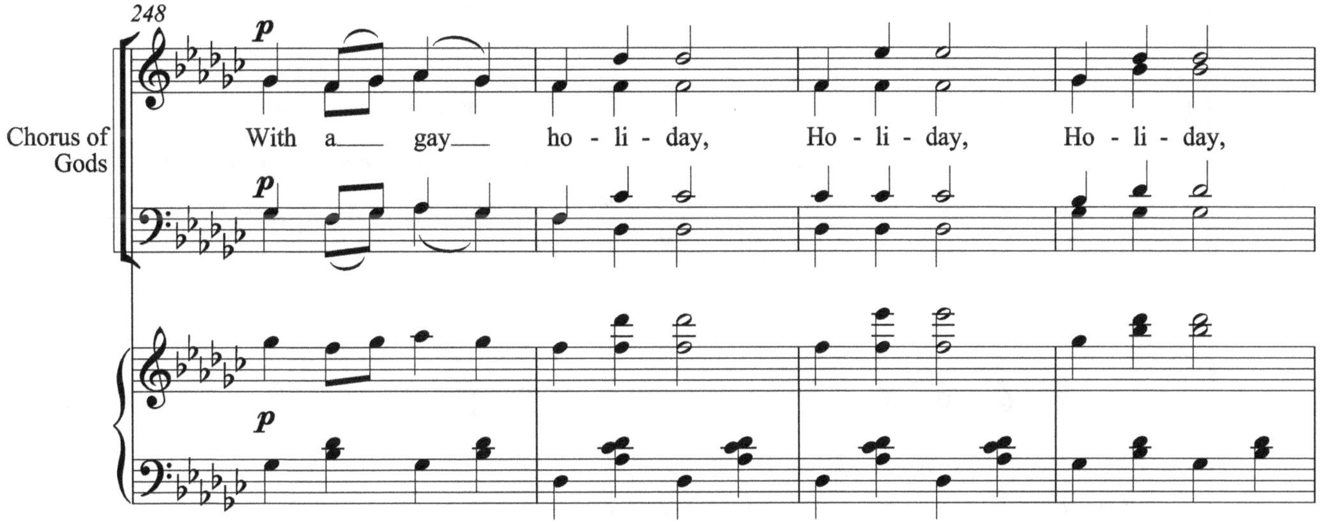
248
Chorus of Gods
With a_ gay_ ho - li - day, Ho - li - day, Ho - li - day,
p

252
Chorus of Gods
All un - known and a - lone, Yes un-known and a - lone.

256
Chorus of Gods
f
We will go Down be - low Down be - low
Chorus of Mortals
f
Here's a pret - ty tale for fu - ture Il - i - ads and Od - y - sseys:

Chorus of Gods: Re - vels rare, What re - vels we will share. Ha ha ha!

Chorus of Mortals: Mor-tals are a - bout to per-son - ate the gods and god-des-ses. Now to set the

Chorus of Gods: We will go___ Down be - low___ All un-known and a-lone, Yes

Chorus of Mortals: world in or - der, we will work in un-i-ty___ Ju - pi - ter's per - plex - i - ty is

270
Chorus of Gods
un - known and a - lone.
We go,
Chorus of Mortals
Thes-pi-s' op-por - tu-ni-ty.
Now to set the world in or - der We will

274
Chorus of Gods
Be - low
We go,
Chorus of Mortals
work in u - ni - ty.
Now to set the world in or - der, We will

278
Chorus of Gods
Be - low
Now we work
cresc
Chorus of Mortals
work in u - ni - ty. Now to set the world in or - der, Now to
cresc
cresc
282
We
We will work in
f
We
set the world in or - der, We will work in
f
f

90

Chorus of
Gods and
Mortals

Ju - pi - ter's per - plex - i - ty is Thes-pis 's Op - por - tu - ni - ty.

The gods, group themselves on rising ground at back and prepare to descend to earth.
The Thespians bid them farewell with a cheer.

CURTAIN

END ACT I

ENTR'ACTE

ACT II

SCENE: The same scene as in Act I, with the exception that in place of the ruins that filled the foreground of the stage, the interior of a magnificent temple is seen, showing the background of the scene of Act I, through the columns of the portico at the back. High throne L.U.E. Low seats below it.

All the substitute gods and goddesses (that is to say, Thespians) are discovered grouped in picturesque attitudes about the stage, eating, drinking, and smoking, and singing the following verses:-

No. VIII
OPENING ACT II (Sillimon & Chorus of Mortals)
Of all symposia

13
18
A
f
Mortals
Of all sym-po - sia the best by half up - pon Ol - ym-pus, here a -
22
Mortals
wait us. We eat Am-bro - sia And nec - tar quaff, It cheers but don't in - e - bri-

Mortals: ate us. We

Mortals: know the fal-la-cies of hu-man food, So please to pass Ol-ym-pian ro-sy. We

Mortals: built up pal-a-ces Where ru-ins stood, And find them much more snug and co-sy. We

96

Mortals | built up__ pal-a-ces where ru - ins__stood And find them much more snug and co - sy.

B *mf*

Sil. | To work and think up here, my dear, Would be the height of

Sil. | fol - ly, So eat and drink, I like to see, Young peo - ple gay and jol - ly. Ol -

55
Sil.
ym-pian food, My love, will please your lips, those ro-sy por - tals, What is the use of be-ing gods, If
61
Sil.
we must work like mor - tals?
Mortals
Ol - ym-pian food, We'll lay long odds, Will please those ro - sy
66
Sil.
What is the use of be - ing gods, If we must work like mor - tals?
Mortals
por - tals. What is the use of be - ing gods, If we must work like mor - tals?
mf

71
f
75
C
Mortals
Of all sym - po - sia the best by half up -
f mf
79
Mortals
pon Ol - ym - pus here a - wait us. We eat Am - bro - sia And nec - tar quaff, It

Mortals: cheers but don't in-e-bri - ate us. We

Mortals: know the fal -la-cies of hu -man food, So please to pass Ol-ym-pian ro - sy. We

Mortals: built up pal-a-ces Where ru - ins stood, And find them much more snug and co - sy. We

Mortals: built up_pal-a-ces where ru - ins stood And find them much more snug and co - sy. We eat Am

Mortals: bro - sia and nec - tar quaff: It don't in - e - bri - ate us. Of all sym_ po - sia the best by_

Exeunt all but NICEMIS, *who is dressed as* DIANA, *and* PRETTEIA, *who is dressed as* VENUS. *They take* SILLIMON's *arm and bring him down.* SILLIMON *carries a Prompt Book.*

Sill.   Bless their little hearts, I can refuse them nothing. Now that I've been elevated to the dazzling heights of Olympian stage-manager I ought to be strict with them and make them do their duty, but I can't. Bless their little hearts, when I see the pretty little craft come sailing up to me with a wheedling smile on their pretty little figure-heads, I can't turn my back on 'em. I'm all bow, though I'm sure I try to be stern!

Prett.   You certainly are a dear old thing.

Sill.   She says I'm a dear old thing! Deputy Venus says I'm a dear old thing!

Nice.   It's her affectionate habit to describe everybody in those terms. I am more particular, but still even I am bound to admit that you certainly are a very dear old thing.

Sill.   Deputy Venus says I'm a dear old thing, and deputy Diana, who is much more particular, endorses it! Who could be severe with such deputy divinities?

Prett.   Do you know, I'm going to ask you a favour!

Sill.   Venus is going to ask me a favour!

Prett.   You see, I am Venus.

Sill.   My dear, No one who saw your face would doubt it.

Nice.   *(aside)* No one who knew her character would.

Prett.   Well Venus, you know, is married to Mars.

Sill.   To Vulcan, my dear, to Vulcan. The exact connubial relation of the different gods and goddesses is a point on which we must be extremely particular.

Prett.   I beg your pardon - Venus is married to Mars.

Nice.   *(aside)* If she isn't married to Mars, she ought to be.

Sill.   Then that decides it - call it married to Mars.

Prett.   Now married to Vulcan or married to Mars, what does it signify?

Sill.   My dear, it's a matter on which I have no personal feelings whatever.

Prett.   So that she is married to some one!

Sill.   Exactly! So that she is married to some one. Call it married to Mars.

Prett.   Now here's my difficulty. Timidon takes the place of Mars, and Timidon is my Father!

Sill.   Then why object to Vulcan?

Prett.   Because Vulcan is my grandfather!

Sill.   But, my dear, what an objection! You are simply playing a part until the real gods return. That's all! Whether you are supposed to be married to your father - or your grandfather, what does it matter? This passion for realism is the curse of the stage!

Prett.   That's all very well, but I can't throw myself into a part, when I have to make love to my father. It interferes with my conception of the character. It spoils the part. *(crying)*

Sill.   Well , well , I'll see what can be done.

Exit PRETTEIA. *Enter* SPARKEION

Sill.   That's always the problem with beginners, they've no imaginative powers. A true artist ought to be superior to such considerations. Well, Nicemis – or rather I should say Diana - what's wrong with you? Don't you like your part either?

Nice.   Oh, immensely! It's great fun.

Sill.   Don't you find it lonely out by yourself all night?

Nice.   Oh, but I'm not alone all night!

Sill.   Well I don't want to ask any injudicious questions - but who accompanies you?

Nice.   Who? Why Sparkeion, of course.

Sill.   Sparkeion? Well, but Sparkeion is Phoebus Apollo. He's the Sun, you know.

Nice.   Of course he is; I should catch my death of cold, in the night air, if he didn't accompany me.

Spark.   My dear Sillimon, it would never do for a young lady to be out alone all night. It wouldn't be respectable.

Sill.   Hmm, there's a good deal of truth in that. But still - the Sun - at night ?- I don't like the idea. *(referring to the prompt book)* The original Diana always went out alone.

Nice.   I hope the original Diana is no rule for me. After all, what does it matter?

Exit NICEMIS

Sill.   To be sure - what does it matter?

Spark.   The sun at night, or in the daytime!

Sill.   So that he shines. I suppose that's all that's necessary. But poor Daphne, what will she say to this?

Spark.   Oh, Daphne can console herself; young ladies soon get over this sort of thing. Did you never hear of the young lady who was engaged to Cousin Robin?

Sill.   Never.

Spark.   Then I'll sing it to you.

No. IX

SONG (Sparkeion)
Little maid of Arcadee

13
Sp.
He was brave and she was fair. Truth, they made a pret - ty pair.
17
mf
Hap-py lit-tle maid - en she Hap-py maid of Ar - ca - dee!
21
mp
Hap-py lit-tle maid-en, she - Hap-py maid of Ar-ca-dee! Hap-py maid of Ar - ca - dee!
cresc
25
mf

29
B
Sp.
Mo - ments fled as mo-ments will Hap - pi - ly en - ough, un-til,
33
p
Sp.
Af- ter, say, a month or two, Ro-bin did as Ro- bins do.
p
37
f
Sp.
Wea-ry of his lo-ver's play, Jil-ted her and went a - way.
f
41
dim
Sp.
Wret-ched lit-tle maid-en she - Wret-ched maid of Ar-ca-dee! Wretch-ed maid of Ar - ca - dee!
dim

To her lit-tle home she crept, There she sat her down and wept,___

Maid-en wept, as maid-ens will, Grew so thin-and__ pale-un-til

Cou - sin__ Rich-ard came to woo! Then a - gain the ro - ses grew!__

Hap-py lit-tle maid-en, she- Hap-py maid of Ar-ca - dee! Hap-py lit-tle maid-en she,

Hap-py maid of Ar-ca-dee! Hap-py maid of Ar - ca-dee!

Exit SPARKEION, *enter* MERCURY.

Sill.   Well, Mercury, my boy, you've had a year's experience of us up here. How do we do it? I think we're rather an improvement on the original gods - don't you?

Mer.   Well, you see, there's a good deal to be said on both sides of the question; you are certainly younger than the original gods, and, therefore, more active. On the other hand, they are certainly older than you, and have, therefore, more experience. On the whole I prefer you, because your mistakes amuse me.

No. X
SONG (Mercury)
Olympus is now in a terrible muddle

Allegro con brio

Merc. *Ol-*

A (m.6)

Merc. ym-pus is now in a ter-ri-ble mud-dle, The dep-u-ty de-i-ties all are at fault; They

(m.10)

Merc. splut-ter and splash like a pig in the pud-dle, And dick-ens a one of 'em's ear-ning his salt.

(m.14)

Merc. For Thes-pis as Jove is a ter-ri-ble blun-der, Too ner-vous and ti-mid too

19

Merc.

ea - sy and weak, When - e - ver he's called on to ligh-ten or thun-der, The thought of it keeps him a -

23

B

Merc.

wake for a week! Then migh-ty Mars has-n't the pluck of a par-rot, When

28

Merc.

left in the dark he will qui-ver and quail; And Vul-can has arms that would snap like a car-rot, Be -

32

Merc.

fore he could drive in a ten pen-ny nail Then Ve-nus-'s freck-les are ve-ry re-pell-ing. And

37

Merc.

Ve-nus should *not* have a squint in her eyes; The lear-ned Min-er-va is weak in her spel-ling, And

41

Merc.

sca-tters her 'H - s' all o-ver the skies.

f

46

C

Merc.

Then Plu-to, in kind-heart-ed ten-der-ness er-ring, Can't make up his mind to let

p

50

Merc.

an-y-one die, The *Times* has a par-a-graph e-ver re-cur-ring:'Re-mark-a-ble in-stance of

54
Merc.
lon-gev - i - ty'
On some it has come as a
58
Merc.
ser - i - ous o - nus, To o - thers it's quite an ad - van - tage in short, While
61
Merc.
ev - 'ry Life Of - fice de - clares a big bo - nus, The poor un - der - ta - kers are all in the court!
65
D
Merc.
Then cu - pid the ra - scal, for - get - ting his trade is To

Merc. *69*

make men and wo-men im - part -ial -ly smart; Will on - ly shoot ar-rows at pret -ty young la-dies, And

Merc. *73*

ne - ver takes aim at a bach - e - lor's heart. The re - sults of this freak, or what-

Merc. *77*

e - ver you term it, Should co - ver the wick - ed young scamp with dis - grace; While

Merc. *80*

ev -'ry young man is as shy as a her-mit, Young la -dies are pop-ping all o - ver the place!

f

Merc.

84

This

E 88

Merc. would-n't much mat-ter for bash-ful and shy men, When skil-ful-ly hand-led, are

91

Merc. cer-tain to fall, A-las that det-er-mined young bach-e-lor Hy-men Re-fu-ses to wed an-y-

95

Merc. bo-dy at all! He swears that Love's flame is the vil-est of ar-sons, And

Merc. *100*

looks up - on mar - riage as quite a mis - take; Now what in the world's to be - come of the par - sons, And

Merc. *104* **Rall**

what of the art - ist who su - gars the cake?

dim

In

F

Merc. *108* **Slower, colla voce**

short you will see from the facts that I'm show - ing The state of the case is ex - ceed ing - ly sad. If

Merc. *112*

Thes - pis -'s peo - ple go on as they're go - ing, Ol - ym - pus will cer - tain - ly go to the bad!

From

(Bass Drum)

ff

Merc. (117) Ju-pi-ter down-wards there is-n't a dab at it All of 'em quib-ble and shuf-fle and shirk; A

Merc. (121, *Meno mosso*, *Fast*) prem-ier in Down-ing Street form-ing a cab-i-net Could-n't find peo-ple less

Merc. (124) fit for their work!

Enter THESPIS

Thes.   Sillimon, you can retire.

Sill.   Sir, I -

Thes.   Don't pretend you can't when I say you can. I've seen you do it - go! (*Exit SILLIMON bowing extravagantly, THESPIS imitates him*). Well, Mercury, I've been in power one year today.

Mer.   One year today. How do you like ruling the world?

Thes.   Like it! Why, it's as straightforward as possible. Why there hasn't been a hitch of any kind since we came up here. Lor-It does make me so wild! The airs you gods and goddesses give yourselves are perfectly sickening. Why it's mere child's play!

Mer.	Very simple, isn't it?
Thes.	Simple? Why I could do it standing on my head!
Mer.	Ah - I daresay you will do it standing on your head-very soon.
Thes.	What do you mean by that Mercury?
Mer.	I mean that when you've turned the world quite topsy-turvy you won't know whether you're standing on your head or your heels.
Thes.	Well, but, Mercury, it's all right at present.
Mer.	Oh yes … as far as we know.
Thes.	Well, but, you know, we know as much as anybody knows; you know; I believe, that the world's still going on?
Mer.	Yes … as far as we can judge , much as usual.
Thes.	Well, then, give the Father of the Gods his due, Mercury. Don't be envious of the Father of the Gods.
Mer.	Well, but you see you leave too much to accident.
Thes.	Well, Mercury, if I do, it's my principle. I am an easy man, and I like to make things as pleasant as possible. What did I do the day we took office? Why I called the company together and I said to them: 'Here we are, you know, gods and goddesses, no mistake about it, the real thing. Well, we have certain duties to discharge, let's discharge them intelligently. Don't let us be hampered by routine and red tape, let's set the original gods an example, and put a liberal interpretation on our duties. If it occurs to any one to try an experiment in his own department, let him try it, if he fails there's no harm done, if he succeeds it is a distinct gain to society. Take it easy,' I said, ' and at the same time, make experiments. Don't hurry your work, do it slowly, and do it well.' And here we are after a twelvemonth, and not a single complaint or a single petition has reached me.
Mer.	No - not yet.
Thes.	What do you mean by, " No, not yet " ?
Mer.	Well, you see, you don't understand how these things work. All the petitions that are addressed by men to Jupiter pass through my hands, and it's my duty to collect them and present them once a year.
Thes.	Oh, only once a year?
Mer.	Only once a year.
Thes.	And the year is up ?
Mer.	Today.
Thes.	Oh, then I suppose there are some complaints?
Mer.	Yes, there are some.

Thes.	*(disturbed).* Oh. Perhaps there are a good many?
Mer.	There are a good many.
Thes.	Oh. Perhaps there are a thundering lot?
Mer.	There are a thundering lot.
Thes.	*(very much disturbed).* Oh!
Mer.	You see you've been taking it so very easy - and so have most of your company.
Thes.	Oh, and who has been taking it easy?
Mer.	All, except those who have been trying "experiments."
Thes.	Well but I suppose the experiments are ingenious?
Mer.	Yes; they are ingenious, but on the whole ill-judged. But it's time to go and summon your court.
Thes.	What for?
Mer.	To hear the complaints. In five minutes they'll all be here.

Exit MERCURY *laughing.*

(At this point it is possible to insert No. X. A DUET, MERCURY & THESPIS " Life on Earth's a clever toy " Please refer to Appendix).

Thes.	*(Very uneasy).* I don't know how it is, but there is something in that young man's manner that suggests that the Father of the Gods has been taking it too easy. Perhaps it would have been better if I hadn't given my company so much scope. I wonder what they've been doing? I think I must curtail their discretion.

Enter DAPHNE

Thes.	Now then, Daphne, what's the matter with you?
Daph.	Well, you know how disgracefully Sparkeion -
Thes.	*(correcting her)* Apollo -
Daph.	Apollo, then - has treated me. He promised to marry me years ago, and now he's married to Nicemis.
Thes.	Now look here. I can't go into that. You're in Olympus now and must behave accordingly. Drop your Daphne – and assume your Calliope.
Daph.	*(mysteriously)* Quite so. That's it!
Thes.	*(puzzled)* Oh - that is it?
Daph.	That is it, Thespis. I am Calliope, the Muse of Fame.
Thes.	Yes…

Daph.	Very good. This morning I was in the Olympian library, and I took down the only book I could find. Here it is.
Thes.	*(taking it)* Lemprière's Classical Dictionary of The Olympian Peerage.
Daph.	Open it at Apollo.
Thes.	*(opens it)* It is done.
Daph.	Read!
Thes.	"Apollo was several times married, among others to Issa, Bolina, Coronis, Chymene, Cyrene, Chione, Acacallis, and Calliope."
Daph.	*(In triumph)* And Calliope.
Thes.	*(Musing).* Ah! I didn't know he was married to them.
Daph.	*(Severely).* Sir! This is the Family edition.
Thes.	Quite so. But in the original version –
Daph.	I go by the Family edition. You couldn't expect a lady to read any other!
Thes.	On no consideration… Then by the Family edition Apollo is your " Husband ".

Enter NICEMIS *and* SPARKEION.

Nice.	Apollo your husband? I beg your pardon, He is my husband.
Daph.	I beg your pardon. He is my husband.
Nice.	Apollo is Sparkeion, and he's married to me.
Daph.	Sparkeion is Apollo, and he's married to me.
Nice.	He's my husband.
Daph.	No, He's your brother.
Thes.	Look here, Apollo, whose husband are you? Don't let's have any rows about it; whose husband are you?
Spark.	Upon my honour I don't know. I'm in a very delicate position, but I'll happily fall in with any arrangement …Thespis may propose!
Daph.	I've just found out that he's my husband, and yet he goes out every night with that 'thing'!
Thes.	Perhaps he's trying an " experiment."
Daph.	I don't like my husband to make " experiments!"
Spark.	The question is, who are we all and what is our relation to one another?

No. XI
QUARTET (Nicemis, Daphne, Sparkeion & Thespis)
You're Diana, I'm Apollo

Allegro con brio

Sp.: You're Di - a - na, I'm Ap - oll - o - And Cal

li - o - pe__ is she.

Daph.: He's your bro - ther,

Nic.: You're an - o - ther. He has

Nic. fair - ly mar - ried me.

Daph. By the rules of this fair spot, I'm his

Nic. By this gol - den wed - ding

Daph. wife and you are not

Nic. ring, I'm his wife and you're a 'thing'.

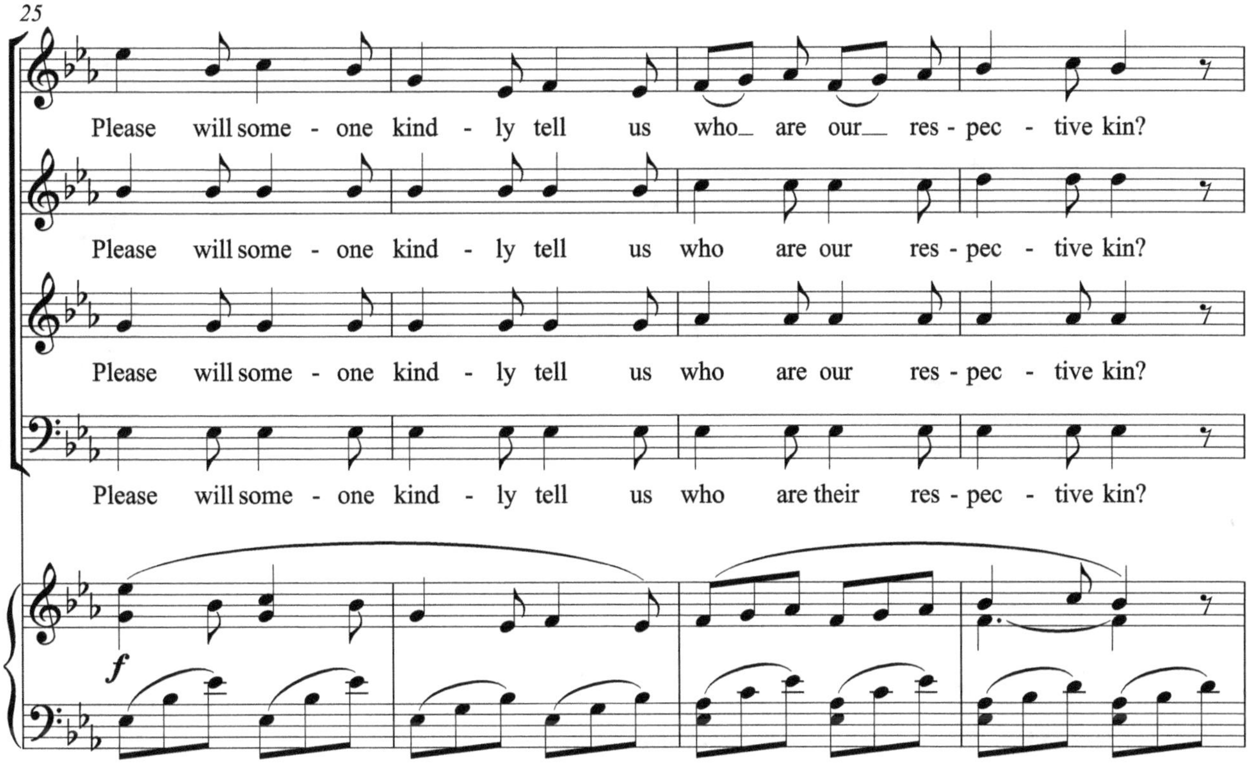
25
Nic.
Please will some - one kind - ly tell us who_ are our_ res - pec - tive kin?
Daph.
Please will some - one kind - ly tell us who are our res - pec - tive kin?
Sp.
Please will some - one kind - ly tell us who are our res - pec - tive kin?
Th.
Please will some - one kind - ly tell us who are their res - pec - tive kin?
f

29
Nic.
All of us are ve - ry jea - lous nei_ ther of_ us will give in.
Daph.
All of us are ve - ry jeal - ous nei - ther of_ us will give in.
Sp.
All of us are ve - ry jeal - ous nei - ther of_ us will give in.
Th.
All of them are ve - ry jea - lous nei - ther of_ them will give in.

122

50
Daph.
bro - ther, I'm his wife, If we go by Lem - pri - ère
Sp.
So she
54
Nic.
He's my
Sp.
is, up - on my life, Real - ly that seems ve - ry fair.
58
Nic.
bro - ther, You're his wife If we go by Lem - pri - ère.

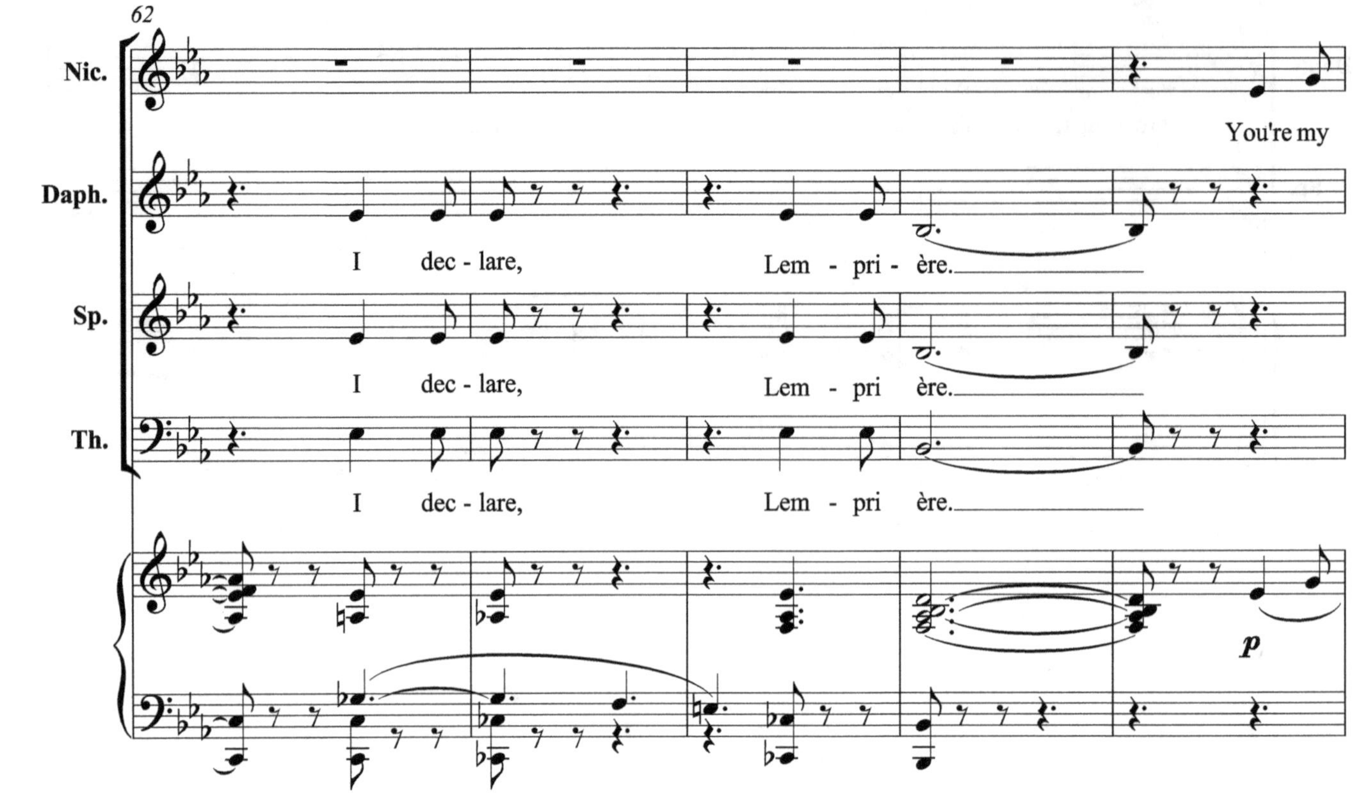
62
Nic.
Daph.
Sp.
Th.
You're my
I dec - lare, Lem - pri - ère.
I dec - lare, Lem - pri ère.
I dec - lare, Lem - pri ère.
p

67
D
Nic.
Daph.
Sp.
hus - band and no o - ther
I'm his wife and you're her
That is true e nough I swear,

72
Nic.
it will sure - ly be un - fair, To de-
Daph.
bro - ther
Sp.
if we go by Lem pri - ère.
77
(Crying)
Nic.
cide by Lem - pri - ère.
Daph.
It will sure - ly be quite fair To de-cide by Lem - pri
82
E
Daph.
ère.
Th.
How you set - tle I don't care Leave it all to Lem - pri - ére,

87
Sp.
How you set - tle he don't care Leave it all to Lem - pri - ère.
Th.
How you set - tle I don't care Leave it all to Lem - pri - ère.
f
91
Th.
(Spoken)
"The verdict:"
F
Meno mosso e colla voce
Parlando
When Spark-eion is Ap - ol - lo, Up in this Ol - ym - pian
96
Th.
clime, Why, Nice - mis, it will fol - low, He's her hus - band for the time. When

Spark - eion turns to mor - tal, Joins once more the sons of

men, He may take you to his por - tal he___ will be your hus - band

G **A tempo**

then. That oh that is my de - ci - sion, 'Cord - ing to my men - tal

112
Sp.
Put an end to all col - li - sion, That oh that is his de - ci - sion.
Th.
vi - sion, Put an end to all col - li - sion, That oh that is my de - ci - sion.

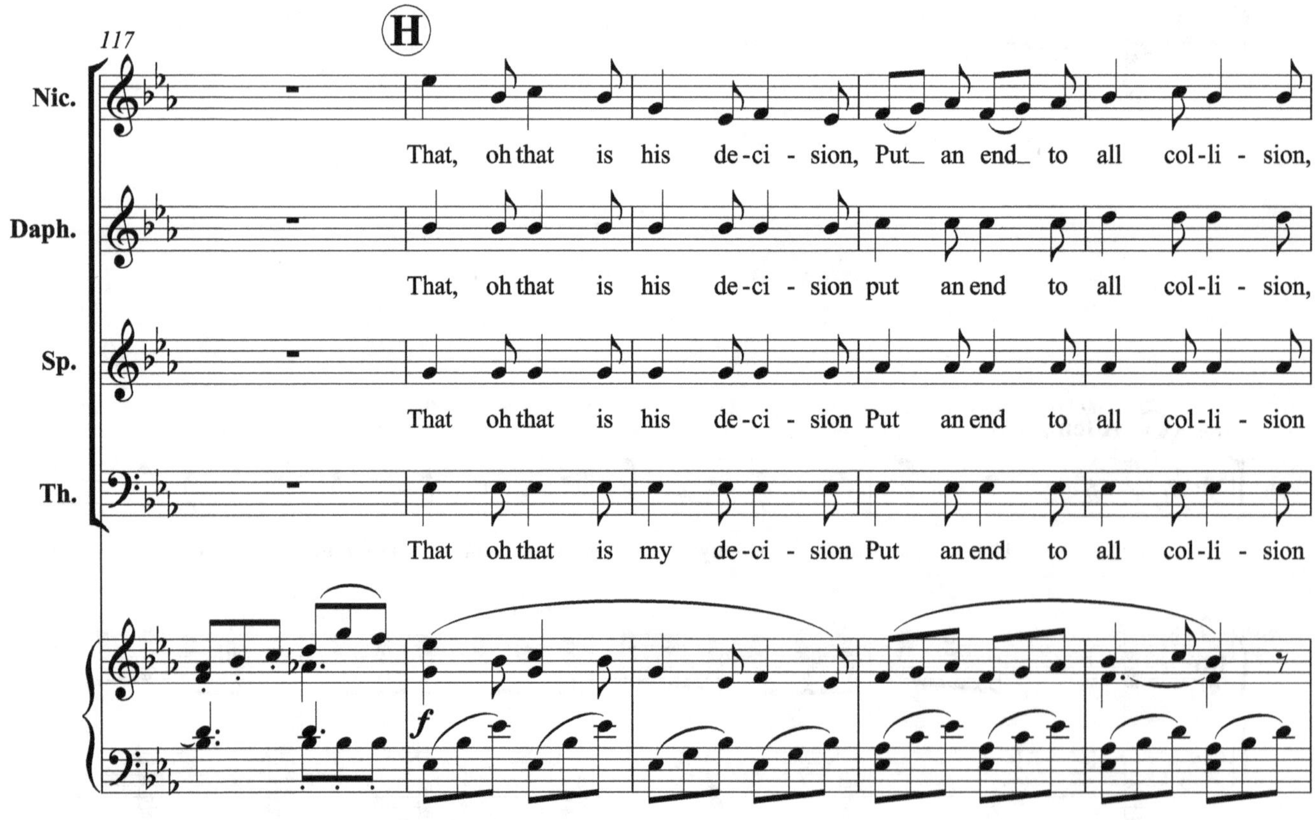
117
H
Nic.
That, oh that is his de - ci - sion, Put an end to all col - li - sion,
Daph.
That, oh that is his de - ci - sion put an end to all col - li - sion,
Sp.
That oh that is his de - ci - sion Put an end to all col - li - sion
Th.
That oh that is my de - ci - sion Put an end to all col - li - sion
f

122
Nic.
That, oh that is his de - ci - sion 'Cor - ding to his men - tal vi - sion,
Daph.
That oh that is his de - ci - sion 'Cor - ding to his men - tal vi - sion,
Sp.
That oh that is his de - ci - sion 'Cor - ding to his men - tal vi - sion,
Th.
That oh that is my de - ci - sion 'Cor - ding to my men - tal vi - sion,
f

126
Nic.
That Oh that, Yes that is his de - ci - sion his de - ci - - - -
Daph.
That, Oh that, Yes that is his de - ci - sion his de - ci - - - -
Sp.
That Oh that, Yes that is his de - ci - sion his de - ci - - - -
Th.
That Oh that, Yes that is my de - ci - sion, my de - ci - - - -

Exeunt SPARKEION *with* DAPHNE *and* NICEMIS *weeping with* THESPIS.

Segue

No. XIa
MELOS (Instrumental)

Thunder & Lightning. Enter JUPITER, APOLLO and MARS, from below, at the back of the stage.
All wear cloaks as disguise and all are masked, they carry umbrellas.

No. XII

TRIO (Mars, Apollo & Jupiter)
Oh rage and fury!

A
17
Mars
Oh rage and fu - ry! Oh shame and sor - row!
Ap.
Oh rage and fu - ry! Oh shame and sor row!
Jup.
Oh rage and fu - ry! Oh shame and sor - row!

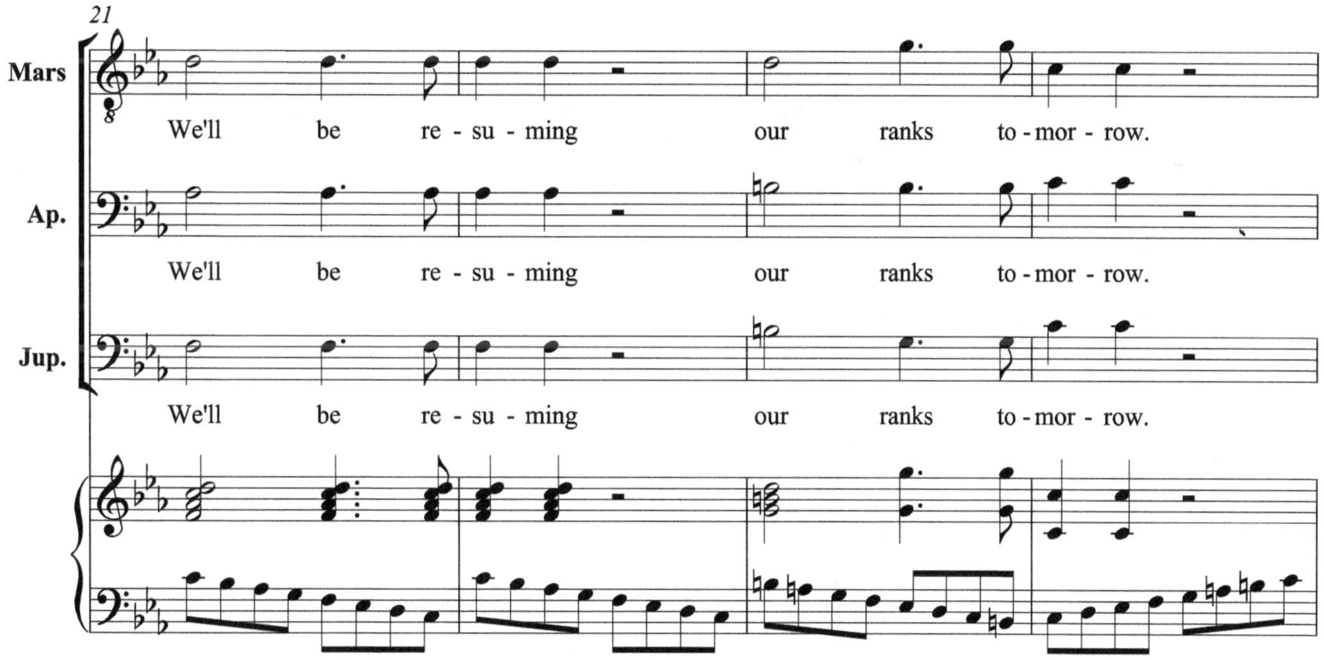
21
Mars
We'll be re - su - ming our ranks to - mor - row.
Ap.
We'll be re - su - ming our ranks to - mor - row.
Jup.
We'll be re - su - ming our ranks to - mor - row.

25
Mars
Since from Ol - ym - pus we have de - par - ted
Ap.
Since from Ol - ym - pus we have de - par - ted
Jup.
Since from Ol - ym - pus we have de - par - ted

29
Mars
We've been dis - trac - ted and bro - ken heart - ed.
Ap.
We've been dis - trac - ted and bro - ken heart - ed.
Jup.
We've been dis - trac - ted and bro - ken heart - ed.

33
Mars
Oh wick - ed Thes - pis! Oh vil - lian scur - vy;
Ap.
Oh wick - ed Thes - pis! Oh vil - lian scur - vy;
Jup.
Oh wick - ed Thes - pis! Oh vil - lian scur - vy;
37
Mars
Through him Ol - ym - pus Is top - sy tur - vy!
Ap.
Through him Ol - ym - pus Is top - sy tur - vy!
Jup.
Through hiim Ol - ym - pus Is top - sy tur - vy!
41
B
Mars
We're com pelled to be si - lent, to grin and to bear it
Ap.
He's
mf

44
Ap.
caused all our sor - row, and now he shall share it
Jup.
Oh where is the mon - ster! A -
47
Mars
For he has a - wa - kened O - lym - pian thun - ders.
Ap.
For he has a - wa - kened O - lym - pian thun - ders.
Jup.
venge all his blun - ders; For he has a - wa - kened O - lym - pian thun - ders.
cresc
C
50
Mars
f
Oh rage and fu - ry! Oh shame and
Ap.
f
Oh rage and fu - ry! Oh shame and
Jup.
f
Oh rage and fu - ry!
f

54
Mars
sor - row! We'll be re - su - ming our ranks to-
Ap.
sor row! We'll be re - su - ming our ranks to-
Jup.
Oh shame and sor - row! We'll be re-sum - ing our ranks to-

58
D Poco più agitato
Mars
mor-row. Oh wi - cked Thes - pis Oh vil - lian
Ap.
mor-row. Oh wi - cked Thes - pis Oh vil - lian
Jup.
mor-row Oh wi - cked Thes - pis oh vil - lian
Poco più agitato
ff

62
Mars
scur - vy, Through him Ol - ym - pus Is top - sy
Ap.
scur - vy, Through him Ol - ym - pus Is top - sy
Jup.
scur - vy, Through him Ol - ym - pus Is top - sy

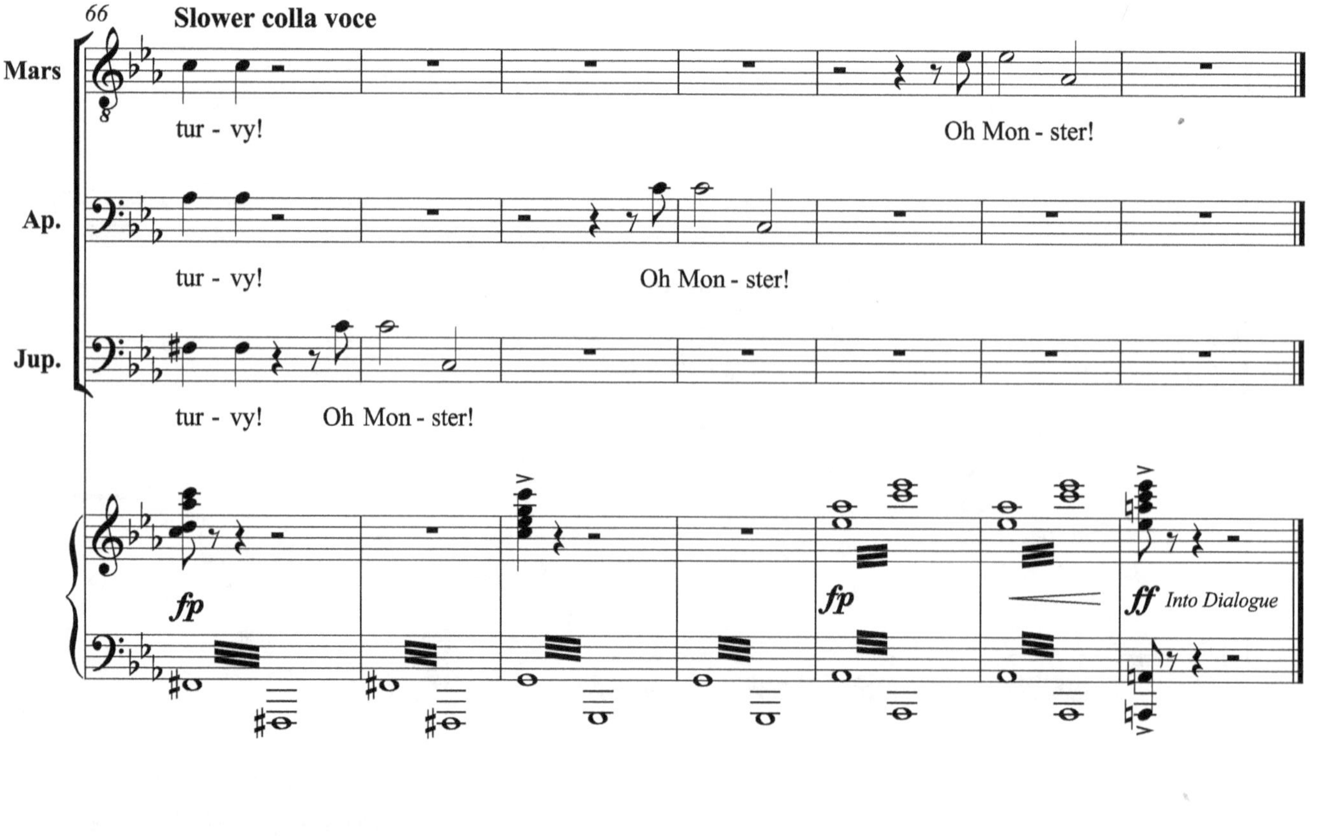
66
Slower colla voce
Mars
tur - vy! Oh Mon - ster!
Ap.
tur - vy! Oh Mon - ster!
Jup.
tur - vy! Oh Mon - ster!
fp
fp
ff Into Dialogue

Enter Mercury.

Mer.   *(In great terror)* Please sir, what have I done sir?

Jup.   What did we leave you behind for?

Mer.   Please sir, that's the question I asked when you went away.

Jup.   Was it not that Thespis might consult you whenever he was in a difficulty?

Mer.   Well, here I've been, ready to be consulted, chockfull of reliable information - running over with celestial maxims - advice gratis ten to four - after twelve, ring the night bell, in cases of emergency.

Jup.   And hasn't he consulted you?

Mer.   Not he - he disagrees with me about everything.

Jup.   He must have misunderstood me. I told him to consult you whenever he was in a fix.

Mer.   He must have thought you said insult. Whenever I open my mouth he jumps down my throat. It isn't pleasant to have a fellow constantly jumping down your throat - especially when he always disagrees with you.It's the sort of thing I can't digest.

Jup.   *(In a rage)* Send him here at once , I'll talk to him.

Enter THESPIS. He is much terrified.

No XIIa
INTERPOLATED RECITATIVE (Mars, Apollo & Jupiter)
Oh Monster!

Jup.   Well Thespis ! Your one year in power is up today.

Ap.   And a nice mess you've made of it.

Mars.   You've deranged the whole scheme of society, Sir.

Thes.   (aside) There's going to be a row! (*aloud and very familiarly*)
My dear boy - I do assure you -

Thes.   I don't know what you allude to. With the exception of getting our scene-painter to run up this temple, because we found the ruins draughty, we haven't touched a thing.

Thes.   My dear fellows, you're distressing yourselves unnecessarily. Look the Court of Olympus is about to assemble to listen to the complaints of the year, if there are any, but there are none, or, well, next to none ... Mercury let the Olympians assemble!

No. XIII (i)

FIRST BALLET DIVERTISSEMENT
(Instrumental)

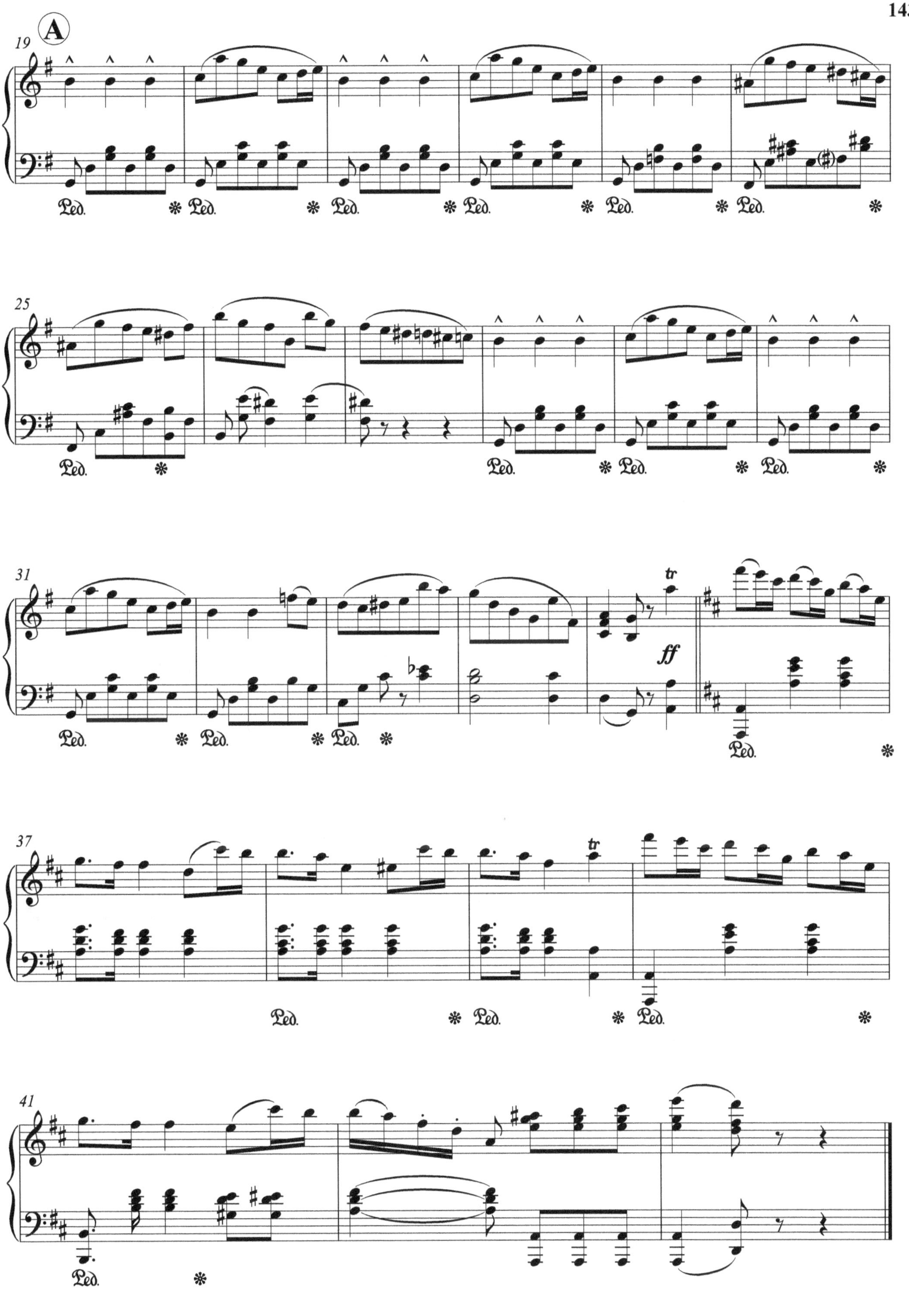
A
19
Ped.
25
31
tr
ff
37
41

No. XIII (ii)

SECOND BALLET DIVERTISSEMENT
(Instrumental)

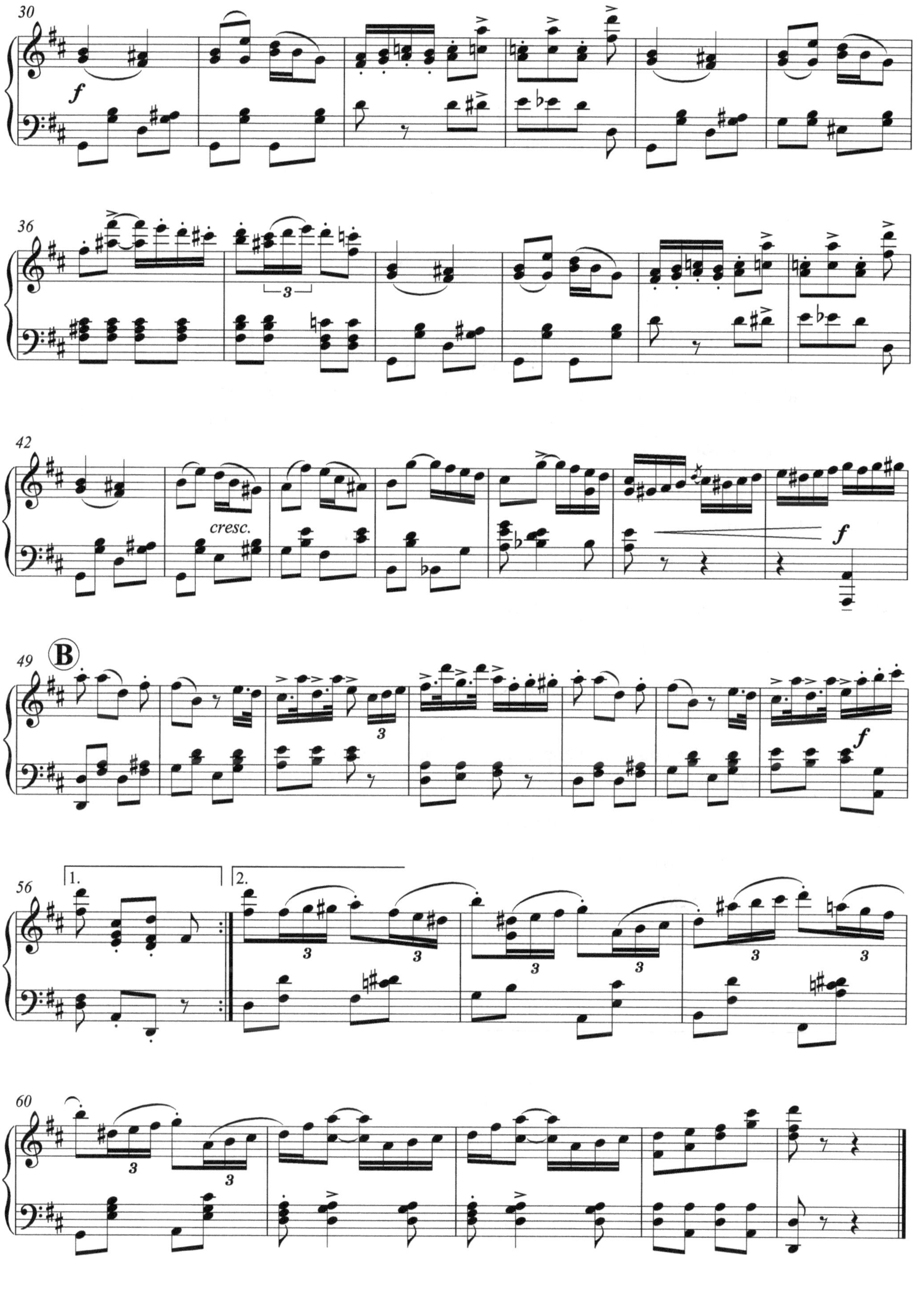
30
f
36
3
42
cresc.
f
49
B
3
f
56
1.
2.
3
60
3

At the end of the dance the characters are all in place for the "Olympian Court" THESPIS takes chair. JUPITER, APOLLO, and MARS, masked, sit below him.

Thes.	Ladies and Gentlemen, I understand that it is usual for the gods to assemble once a year to listen to mortal petitions.It doesn't seem to me to be a good plan, as work is liable to accumulate; but as I'm particularly anxious not to interfere with Olympian precedent, but to allow everything to go on as it has always been accustomed to - why, we'll say no more about it.
	(aside to Jupiter) But how shall I account for your presence?
Jup.	Say that we are Gentlemen of the Press.
Thes.	Ah Good Idea.That all our proceedings may be open and above-board I have communicated with the most influential members of the Athenian press, and I beg to introduce to your notice three of it's most distinguished members. They bear marks emblematic of the anonymous character of modern journalism. Now then, if you're all ready we will begin.

(MERCURY brings in a tremendous bundle of petitions).

Mer.	Here is the agenda.
Thes.	What's that? -The petitions?
Mer.	Some of them. *(opens one and reads)*. Ah, I thought there'd be a row about it.
Thes.	Why, what's wrong now?
Mer.	Why, it's been a wet Friday in November for the last six months and the Athenians are tired of it.
Thes.	There's no pleasing some people. This craving for perpetual change is the curse of the country. Friday's a very nice day.
Mer.	So it is, but a Friday six months long! - it gets monotonous.
Jup., Ap., & Mars.	It's perfectly ridiculous.
Thes.	It shall all be explained . Cymon!
Cymon.	*(As Father Time with the usual attributes, hourglass and scythe)*. Sir!
Thes.	*(Introducing him to the three gods)* Allow me - Father Time - rather young at present but even Time must have a beginning. Now then, Father Time, what's this about a wet Friday in November for the last six months?
Cym.	Well, the fact is, I've been trying an experiment. Seven days in the week is an awkward number. It can't be halved. Two's into seven won't go.
Thes.	*(Tries it on his fingers)* Quite so - quite so.
Cym.	So I abolished Saturday.
Jup., Ap.,. & Mars.	*(rising)* Oh but this is an outrage !...

Thes.	Do be quiet! He's a very intelligent young man and knows what he's about. So you abolished Saturday. And how did you find it answer?
Cym.	Admirably, only Sunday refused to take its place. Sunday comes after Saturday - Sunday won't go on duty after Friday, Sunday's principles are very strict- and that's where my experiment sticks.
Thes.	Well, but why November?
Cym.	December can't begin till November has finished. November can't finish because I've abolished Saturday. So there again my experiment sticks.
Thes.	Well, but why wet? Come now, why wet?
Cym.	Oh, that's your fault. You turned the rain on six months ago, and you forgot to turn it off again.
Jup., Ap.,. & Mars. (Rising)	Oh this is monstrous!
Sill.	Order, order. Decorum in the Olympian Court !
Thes.	Gentlemen, pray be seated. (to the others) The liberty of the Press! It is easily settled. Athens has had a wet Friday in November for the last six months. Let them have a blazing Tuesday in July for the next twelve.
Jup., Ap.,. & Mars.	But this is quite preposterous…
Sill.	Order! Order!
Thes.	Now then, whats the next article.
Mer.	Here's a petition from the Peace Society. They complain that there are no more battles.
Mars.	*(springing up)* What! What was that ?
Jupiter & Ap. (shouting down his Ear Trumpet)	NO MORE BATTLES!
Mars.	NO! This must not be. Battles have been fought for thousands of…
Thes.	Quiet there! Good dog – So-Ho. Timidon!
Tim.	*(as MARS)* Here Sir.
Thes.	What's this about there being no more battles?
Tim.	I've abolished battles Sir; it's an experiment.
Thes.	Abolished battles?
Tim.	Yes, you told us on taking office to remember two things, to try experiments and to take it easy. I found I couldn't take it easy while there were any battles to attend to, so I tried an experiment and abolished battles. And then I took it easy. The Peace Society ought to be very much obliged to me.
Mer.	Oh very much Obliged to you! For now that battles have been abolished, War is universal!

Tim.   War universal?

Mer.   Now that nations can't fight, no two of 'em are on speaking terms. The dread of fighting was the only thing that kept them civil to each other.

Thespis   Then let battles be restored and peace reign supreme. Next !

Mer.   *(reads)* Here's a petition from the associated wine merchants of Mytilene.

Thes.   Well, and what's wrong with the associated wine merchants of Mytilene? Are there no grapes this year?

Mer.   Plenty of grapes; more than usual.

Thes.   *(to the gods)* You observe, there is no deception here ; there are more than usual.

Mer.   There are plenty of grapes, only they are full of ginger beer.

Jup., Ap.,. & Mars. Oh, I say!

(Rising. They are put down by Sillimon).

Thes.   Bacchus !

Tips.   Here !

Thes.   There seems to be something unusual with the grapes of Mytilene; they only grow ginger beer!

Tips.   And a very good thing too.

Thes.   It's very nice in its way, but it is not what one looks for from grapes.

Tips.   Beloved master, a week before we came up here you insisted on my taking the pledge. By doing so you rescued me from my otherwise inevitable misery. I cannot express my thanks. Embrace me! *(Attempts to embrace him)*.

Thes.   Get out, don't be a fool. Look here, you know, you're the god of wine.

Tips.   I am.

Thes.   Well, do you consider it consistent with your duty as the god of wine to make grapes yield nothing but ginger beer?

Tips.   Do you consider it consistent with my duty as a total abstainer, to grow anything stronger than ginger beer?

Thes.   But your duty as the god of wine-

Tips.   In every respect in which my duty as the god of wine can be discharged consistently with my duty as a total abstainer, I will discharge it. But when the functions clash, everything must give way to the pledge.

Thes.   Oh you confounded fool! This can be arranged. We can't give over the wine this year, but at least we can improve the ginger beer. Let all the ginger be extracted from it immediately.

Merc.	I'm afraid that is going to be rather difficult as the harvest will take some time. You see, Deputy Ceres has caused all the crops to grow topsy-turvy and the grapes will have to be dug out like potatoes.
Thes.	*(Collapses into chair)* Oh no!
Merc.	Here's another, Deputy Venus has caused all babies to be born grown up. This wouldn't be so bad, but its playing havoc with the birth rate !
Prett.	*(timidly)* It was an experiment…
Merc.	Do you want any more? *(Mercury gives a huge bundle of petitions to Thespis)*

The Olympian Court erupts into chaos.

No. XIV

FINALE ACT II

(Nicemis, Daphne, Sparkeion, Timidon, Thespis, Sillimon, Mars, Apollo, Jupiter & Chorus of Gods and Mortals)

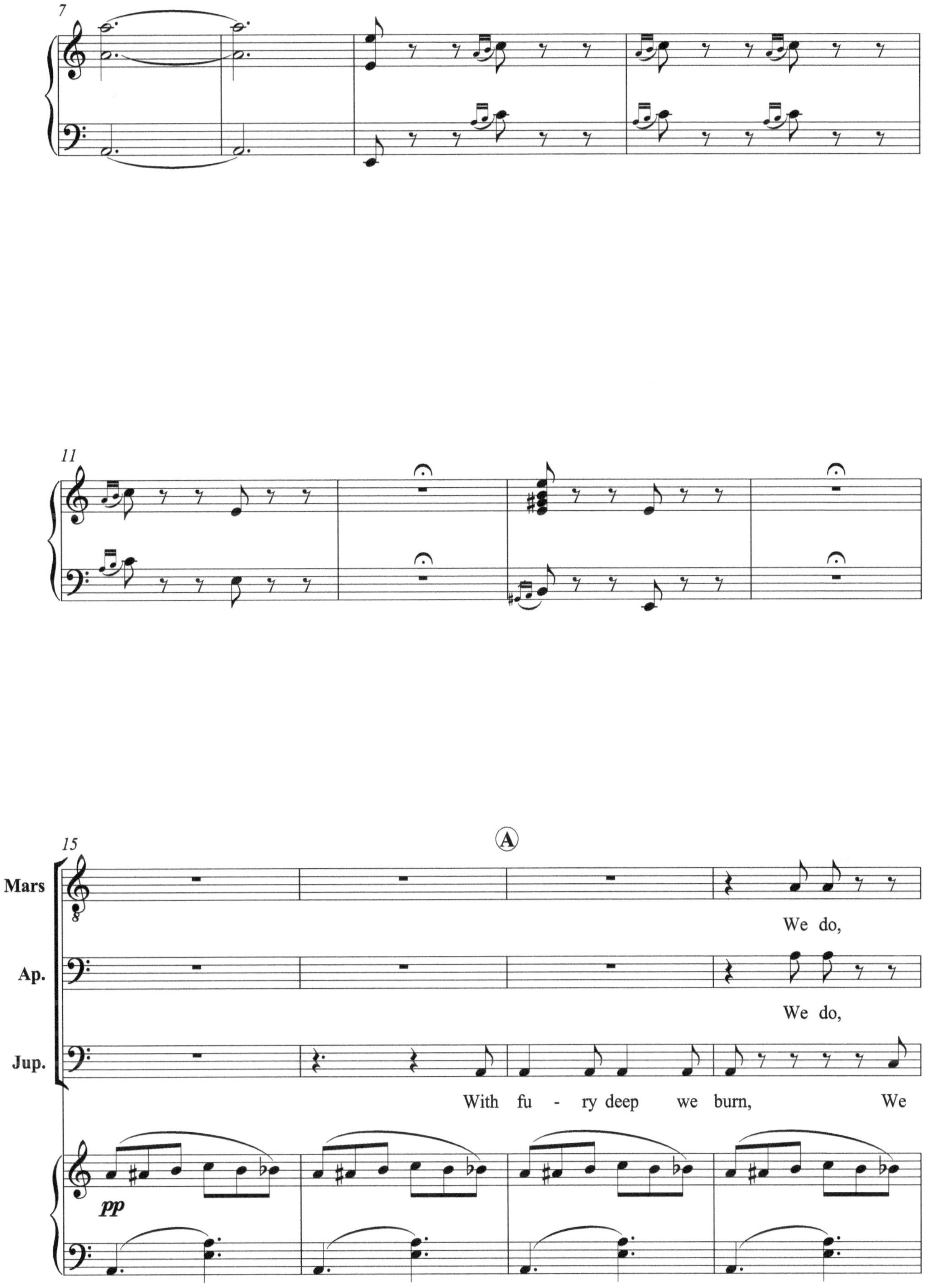
7
11
15
A
Mars
Ap.
Jup.
We do,
We do,
With fu - ry deep we burn, We
pp

19
Mars
we do, Your i - dle-ness and lack of sense, Has
Ap.
we do, Your i - dle-ness and lack of sense, Has
Jup.
fume with smo - thered rage, Your i - dle-ness and lack of sense, Has

23
Mars
caused a fear - ful con - se-quence, We've had en-ough, now get you hence, It's
Ap.
caused a fear - ful con - se-quence,
Jup.
caused a fear - ful con - se-quence,

27
Mars
time to leave the stage, It's time to leave the stage For
Ap.
It is! For
Jup.
It is! For

31
Mars
This must-n't be, and this won't do, The world has had e - nough of you, For
Ap.
This must-n't be, and this won't do, The world has had e - nough of you, For
Jup.
This must-n't be, and this won't do, The world has had e - nough of you, For

Mars: this must-n't be and this won't do, Yes this must-n't be and this won't do No,

Ap.: this must-n't be and this won't do, Yes this must-n't be and this won't do No,

Jup.: this must-n't be and this won't do, Yes this must-n't be and this won't do No,

Mars: This won't do!_____

Ap.: This won't do!_____

Jup.: This won't do!_____

44
Moderato
S+A
p
B with indignance
Mortals
Great Jove, this in -ter fer -ence, Is more than we can stand;
mp
48
Mars
mf
What fools these mor-tals be, Your
Ap.
mf
What fools these mor-tals be, Your
Jup.
mf
What fools these mor-tals be, Your
Mortals
Of them make a clear -ance, With your ma -jes -tic hand.

Mars: threats to us ring hol-low, I'm Mars!

Ap.: threats to us ring hol-low, And I'm Ap-

Jup.: threats to us ring hol-low, I'm Ju-pi-ter!

Ap.: -ol-lo!

Con Forza

Allegro vivace

59
C
Nic.
Daph.
Sp.
Tim.
Sil.
p
The
The
The
Ju - pi - ter, Mars and A - poll - o, Have quit-ted the dwell-ings of men;
Ju - pi - ter, Mars and A - poll - o, Have quit-ted the dwell-ings of men;
63
o - ther gods quick-ly will fol - low, And what will be-come of us then?
o - ther gods quick-ly will fol - low, And what will be-come of us then?
o - ther gods quick-ly will fol - low, And what will be-come of us then?
Oh
Oh

67
Nic.
Oh
Daph.
Oh
Sp.
Oh
Tim.
par-don us, Jove and A - poll - o, Par-don us Ju - pi - ter, Mars;
Sil.
par-don us, Jove and A - poll - o, Par-don us Ju - pi - ter, Mars;

71
Nic.
see us in mi - se - ry wal - low, Cur-sing our ter - ri - ble stars.
Daph.
see us in mi - se - ry wal - low, Cur-sing our ter - ri - ble stars.
Sp.
see us in mi - se - ry wal - low, Cur-sing our ter - ri - ble stars.

75
D
Gods
Ju-pi-ter, Mars and A - poll - o, Have quit-ted the dwell-ings of men; The o-ther gods quick-ly will
Mortals
Ju-pi-ter, Mars and A - poll - o, Have quit-ted the dwell-ings of men; The o-ther gods quick-ly will

80
Gods
fol - low, And what will be-come of them then?
Mortals
fol - low, And what will be-come of us then? Oh par-don us, Jove and A - poll - o,

85
Gods
Oh see them in mi - se - ry wal - low, Cur - sing their ter - ri - ble
Mortals
par - don us Ju - pi - ter, Mars;
90
Gods
stars.
ff
Oh
ff
Mortals
ff
Oh, par - don us Jove and A - pol - lo, Par - don us Ju - pi - ter, Mars; Oh
ff
ff

Gods: see them in mi-se-ry wal_ low, cur-sing their ter-ri-ble, ter-ri-ble stars!

Mortals: see us in mi-se-ry wal_ low, cur-sing our ter-ri-ble, ter-ri-ble stars!

104
E quasi recit
Gods
Mortals
One god - Solo
Let them re-main, they beg of us plea-ding-ly!
Let us re-main, we beg of you plea-ding-ly!
sf

109
Gods
Mortals
One god - soli
Life on Ol-y-mpus suits them ex-ceed-ing-ly!
Another god - soli
Life on Ol-y-mpus suits them ex-ceed-ing-ly!
Life on Ol-y-mpus suits us ex-ceed-ing-ly!
sf

113
Gods
Four gods
Let 'em re-main, they pray in hu-mil-i-ty,
Let 'em re-main, they pray in hu-mil-i-ty,
Mortals
Let us re-main, we pray in hu-mil-i-ty,
sf
117
Gods
Tutti chorus of gods
If they have shown some lit-tle a-bil-i-ty...
Mortals
If we have shown some lit-tle a-bil-i-ty...
sf

121 **Marcato e pesante (in 4)** Grave *f* Ⓕ

Jup.

Enough, your reign has end - ed; Up

ff

mf

p

127

Jup.

on this sa - cred hill. Let him be ap - pre - hen - ded, And

mf

p

mp

131 **Rall**

Jup.

learn our aw - ful will.

p

Ped.

❋

134 Ⓖ **Colla voce**

Jup.

A way to earth, con-temp-ti-ble com-e-dians, And hear our curse, be-fore we set you free.

139
Jup.
Ye shall all be em-i-nent tra-ge-dians, Whom no-one e-ver, ev-er, goes to see!
Tutti
Gods and Mortals, with Principals
p
We
They
144
H Meno mosso e cantabile
go to earth, con-temp-ti-ble co-me-dians, We hear his curse, be - fore he sets us free,
They them
148
Rallentando
We shall all be e - mi-nent tra-ge-dians, Whom no one e-ver, e-ver goes to
They
p

152
I Adagio
Sp.
Sil.
Tutti
p
Whom no - one
Whom no - one
see!
157
Rallentando
Sp.
Th.
Sil.
Tutti
pp
mf
Whom no - one
E-ver e-ver goes to see...
E-ver e-ver goes to see... Now
E-ver e-ver goes to see...
E-ver e-ver goes to see...

162
J Colla voce
Th.
here you see the ar-rant fol-ly, Of do-ing your best to make things jol-ly. I'veruled the world like a
mp
167
Th.
chap in his sen-ses; Ob-serve the ter-ri ble con-se-quen-ces. Great Ju-pi-ter, whom
171
Th.
no-thing plea-ses, Splut-ters and swears and kicks up bree-zes, And sends us home, in a mood a-ven-gin' In
In Tempo Allegro
176
Th.
doub-le quick time like a rail-road en-gine. And
f

this he does with-out com-punc-tion, Be-cause I have dis-charged with unc tion, A

high - ly com - pli - ca - ted func-tion Com ply - ing with his own in - junc-tion.

And

this he does with-out com-punc-tion, Be cause he has dis-charged with unc-tion A

192

Tutti

high - ly com - pli - ca - ted func - tion, Com - ply - ing with his own in - junc - tion. And

mf

196 Ⓛ

Th.

A

mf

Tutti

this he does with - out com - punc - tion Be - cause he has dis - charged with unc - tion A

mf

200
cresc
Th.
high - - ly com - - pli
cresc
high - - ly com - - pli - -
Tutti
cresc
Fol did-dle lol did-dle lol did-dle lol did-dle lol did-dle lol did-dle lol did-dle lol did-dle
cresc
204
Th.
ca - - ted func
ca - - ted func - - - - -
Tutti
Fol did-dle lol did-dle lol lol lay, Fol did-dle lol did-dle lol lol lay,

The gods drive the Thespians away.
The Thespians prepare to descend the mountain as the Curtain falls.

APPENDIX
Onstage Percussion for No. 6 – Thespis & Chorus
I once knew a chap

In the 2008 Normansfield production, we decided that it would be suitably "authentic" to incorporate stage percussion 'train effects' at certain points during Thespis' Act I patter song. This was realised by hand held instruments played by members of the chorus, and proved to be a successful device in performance. For those seeking to stage *Thespis* this is of course an optional directorial choice, and in any case, performers are perfectly free to create their own ideas.

We thought it might be useful, however, to explain how we used stage percussion at Normansfield for those who wish to follow a template, find a starting point for their own ideas, or for those who simply wish to imagine it all taking place when reading through the score.

We used five instruments, each played by a member of the chorus and which would have been available in the 1870's: two train guard's whistles of differing pitch; two train (ship's) bells of differing pitch, and sandpaper blocks. We decided that overuse would have had a negative effect both on the song and the poor soloist and so kept each percussive entry as precise as possible.

The first entry was a simple dialogue between two train whistles, starting at bar 46:

At Letter Ⓓ we introduced sandpaper blocks, played until the end of the page:

From bar 107, the four bar instrumental section (the fanfare-like motif itself is designed to reflect the whistle of a steam train) included the following stage percussion accompaniment:

After the final cadence of the piece, the train bells sounded 'all aboard', choreographed of course and in rhythm:

APPENDIX
A Duet for Thespis & Mercury

This duet for Thespis and Mercury is an optional addition to the version that played at Normansfield in 2008. In preparing our material for publication and having had a chance to reflect on *Thespis* in actual performance, it struck me that there is something slightly flawed about the structure of Act Two. From a dramatic and a musical point of view it seems odd that the two most important characters in *Thespis* (Mercury and Thespis himself), never have a musical number together. Or indeed that Thespis has no solo number in the second half.

So in the spirit of the 1875 proposed re- write, I decided that this publication gives us the chance to offer a partial remedy in the form of the Duet which follows. It is of course taken from *HMS Pinafore* and seems apt in the sense that this duet in its original context is full of warning that things are about to change for one character. Likewise in our partially re-written version (lyrics courtesy of Chris Crowcroft) Mercury cryptically hints to Thespis that all is not going quite as well down on earth as he would like to think and that Jove's return and demotion from Gods to mortals is imminent.

Its suggested placement is indicated in the vocal score and comes at the end of the Act Two dialogue scene between Thespis and Mercury.
Cue line: *Merc. "In five minutes they'll all be here."*

INTERPOLATED No Xa
DUET (Mercury & Thespis)
Life on earth's a clever toy
Lyrics by Chris Crowcroft after W.S.Gilbert

Mercury: Life on earth's a cle - ver toy,

Merc.: Wind it gen - tly, watch with joy. Wind it cru - dely- sad mis-take,

Merc.: Watch it qui - ver, watch it break.

Th.: Ve - ry true, So it do.

14
Merc.
Gods and mor - tals- hap - py race. Work to - ge - ther, live in grace.
p
18
Merc.
Work at odds, then watch the fun, Eve - ry - thing be -
21
Merc.
comes un - done.
Th.
So it may As you say.
ff

Merc. (m. 25, A): Ju - pi-ter is watch-ing still, do -ings on this heavn'-ly hill. Gild the li - ly if you will,

Merc. (m. 31): Yet it lasts a mo - ment's fill.

Th.: Yes I know, That is so.

Th. (m. 35, B): Though to catch your drift I'm stri - ving, It is ha - zy- it is ha - zy;

Th. I don't see at what you're driving: Am I lazy? Am I lazy?

C

Merc. Doubts and dan - gers o'er_ him_steal-ing To con-clu - sion un - app - ea-ling-

Th. Doubts and dan - gers o'er_ me_steal-ing To con-clu - sion un - app - ea - ling-

Merc. Is there some - thing I'm con - ceal - ing? That is so!

Th. Is there some - thing he's con - ceal - ing? Yes I know

52 (D)

Th. Since my act-ing's ra-ther cle-ver, I could play this role for e-ver.

p

56

Th. Give it hot and give it strong- Play the part the whole night long.

60

Merc. If you must, Go for bust!

ff

63

Th. Shout is of-ten good as sing: With con-vic-tion, that's the thing.

p

Th. Watch your back for foul up-stag-ing, Watch the wings for promp-ter rag-ing.

Merc. So it be, fre - quent - lee.

Th. Act-ing's a bi - zarre pro-fess-ion, Tan - ta-mount to sheer ob-sess-ion-

Th. Play your night-ly in - ter-cess-ion Court the pub-lic, catch the'fesh - ion'.

180

96
Merc.
Th.
Gods to-day but men to- mor - row? That is so.
Gods to-day but men to-mor - row? Yes I know
100
H
Though mys-tic tone we do bor-row, He shall
Though a mys - tic tone we bor-row, I shall learn the
p
103
learn the truth with sor - row. He shall
truth with sor - row; Gods to - day but

ORCHESTRAL PARTS HIRE

This performing version of *Thespis* has its own orchestral parts that are available to hire. These have been specifically arranged and orchestrated by Timothy Henty for this version (with rehearsal figures and bar numbers matching this vocal score). Application to perform the piece must first be made to Anthony Baker who can be contacted via his website *www.anthonybaker.net.* Thereafter, orchestral parts can be hired from Timothy Henty. A hire quote and terms are available on request.

The instrumentation is as follows:

1 FLUTE (doubles Piccolo)
1 OBOE
1 CLARINET IN B♭ AND A
1 BASSOON
1 HORN IN F
1 TRUMPET IN B♭ AND A
1 TROMBONE
1 PERCUSSION
2 Timpani, Snare Drum, Bass Drum, Cymbals, Triangle
STRINGS: VIOLIN I & II, VIOLA, VIOLONCELLO AND DOUBLE BASS
OPTIONAL: STRING 'BUMPER' KEYBOARD PART
INCLUDED: 'CONDUCTOR'S' VOCAL SCORE

Whilst it is possible to perform *Thespis* with an orchestra of 13 players, the arranger strongly advises the use of an expanded string section where possible. A standard hire package includes one part per string section but additional string parts can be sent on request.

Alternatively, or in addition, there is an optional string 'bumper' keyboard part. Please note that this is *not* a straight reduction of the string parts and so does not work on its own, but instead plays in support of the string quintet to achieve a more equitable balance in the pit.

BIOGRAPHIES

Anthony Baker is best known as a Stage Designer and Director for Opera in a career which began in 1989. He trained at the Central School of Art and Design, London. Past credits include operas across four centuries, at the Royal Opera, Covent Garden, WNO and Opera North; at Garsington and Drottningholm; the Liceu, Barcelona, Rome Opera, Teatro Communale di Bologna; New York City Opera, Santa Fe Opera, Los Angeles Opera; The Dallas Opera, Royal Opera, Copenhagen, Grand Theatre de Geneve; and the Australian Opera. He has been a Visiting Professor in Stage Design at the University of Washington, Seattle and at the Central School of Speech and Drama London. His passion for Gilbert & Sullivan is longstanding, as director, designer and performer. He lives in London.

Photo Samantha Cliffe

Timothy Henty is a British conductor. He studied at the Royal College of Music in London under Neil Thomson as a Foundation Scholar, winning the Tagore Gold Medal – the College's highest award presented to him by HRH The Prince of Wales. He now conducts a diverse repertoire with leading ensembles in the UK and abroad, such as the Royal Liverpool Philharmonic, the Malmö Opera and the RTÉ Concert orchestras; the Holland Symfonia and the Orchestra of the Royal Opera House Covent Garden, where he made his debut at age 24. Known for his performances of British music, he made his first appearance at the International Gilbert and Sullivan Festival, Buxton, in 2009. He lives in Surrey, England, with his wife Louise.

www.ingramcontent.com/pod-product-compliance
Lightning Source LLC
Chambersburg PA
CBHW080554090426
42735CB00016B/3234